CLASSIC SERMONS
ON
PRAISE

CLASSIC SERMONS

ON

PRAISE

Compiled by
Warren W. Wiersbe

HENDRICKSON PUBLISHERS

Classic Sermons on Praise
Hendrickson Publishers, Inc. edition
ISBN 1-56563-158-7

This edition is published by special arrangement with
and permission of Kregel Publications. Copyright © 1994
by Kregel Publications, a division of Kregel, Inc. P.O. Box
2607, Grand Rapids, MI 49501.

Printed in the United States of America

CONTENTS

LIST OF SCRIPTURE TEXTS

PREFACE

THE *KREGEL CLASSIC SERMONS SERIES* is an attempt to assemble and publish meaningful sermons from master preachers about significant themes.

These are *sermons*, not essays or chapters taken from books about themes. Not all of these sermons could be called "great," but all of them are *meaningful*. They apply the truths of the Bible to the needs of the human heart, which is something that all effective preaching must do.

While some are better known than others, all of the preachers whose sermons I have selected had important ministries and were highly respected in their day. The fact that a sermon is included in this volume does not mean that either the compiler or the publisher agrees with or endorses everything that the man did, preached, or wrote. The sermon is here, because it has a valued contribution to make.

These are sermons about *significant* themes. The pulpit is no place to play with trivia. The preacher has thirty minutes in which to help mend broken hearts, change defeated lives, and save lost souls; and he can never accomplish this demanding ministry by distributing homiletical tidbits. In these difficult days we do not need "clever" pulpiteers who discuss the times; we need dedicated ambassadors who will preach the eternities.

The reading of these sermons can enrich your spiritual life. The studying of them can enrich your skills as an interpreter and expounder of God's truth. However God uses these sermons in your life and ministry, my prayer is that His Church around the world will be encouraged and strengthened by them.

WARREN W. WIERSBE

A New Song

Clovis Gillham Chappell (1882–1972) was one of American Methodism's best-known and most effective preachers. He pastored churches in Washington, DC; Dallas and Houston, Texas; Memphis, Tennessee; and Birmingham, Alabama. His pulpit ministry drew great crowds. He was especially known for his biographical sermons that made biblical characters live and speak to our modern day. He published about thirty volumes of sermons.

This message was taken from *Sermons from the Psalms*, published by Abingdon-Cokesbury Press.

Clovis Gillham Chappell

1

A NEW SONG

He hath put a new song in my mouth (Psalm 40:3).

HERE IS A word to interest the most listless. However drowsy we are, this text ought to rouse us into eager wakefulness. However hopeless we are, it ought to startle us into glad expectation. It is a word that is needed in every age. It is especially needed by the jaded generation of which we are a part.

Life has grown old for many of us. In spite of all our facilities for thrills, we are finding the business of living rather stale and unexciting. "What has been will be, and there is no new thing under the sun," said a tired and bored cynic many years ago. To this pessimistic declaration many of us are ready to give a hearty "Amen." Instead of finding new songs we have found old yawns. Or if there has been any music at all, too often it has been a jarring jazz that has left us the more weary and disillusioned. But here is one who has discovered a new song. Life for him is not in the sear and yellow leaf; it is in the full flush of spring. He has therefore a story to tell that we greatly need to hear.

1. The Source of This New Song and Its Fountain of Inspiration

What is the source of this new song? From what fountain of inspiration does it flow?

This song is not a child of chance. No more is it a creature of circumstances. It is not merely a song of youth, for instance. There is nothing to indicate that this poet is singing simply because he is brushing the dewy flowers of life's morning. Even though such were the case, we know well enough that youth cannot always be depended upon to be an inspirer of song. Sometimes youth sings, but very

11

often it does not. Many of our youth today seem to find life quite as drab and insipid as those of us who are in middle life, or as those who are nearing the sunset. In fact, some of the most weary and listless souls that I meet are young men and women who have not yet left their twenties. Some even seem thoroughly fed up on life who are on the springtime side of twenty. Therefore, to look to youth as a sure inspiration of song is to look to a source that is thoroughly unreliable.

No more does this song have its rise in the hills of prosperity and worldly success. There is no slightest hint, in the first place, that this poet had found either fame or fortune. Nor is there anywhere proof that the prosperous are more songful than the failures. Some years ago I was entertained in the home of a man whose wealth amounted to many millions. During the afternoon the husband and wife took me for a drive in and around the city. When we came back, as we were getting out of the car, in spite of the fact that company was present, the wife burst into tears. She was a woman of an assured place in society. She seemed to possess all that heart could wish. She lived in a palace, yet, as I have thought of that home in after years, I have thought of it not so much as a place of songs as a place of sobs. We can safely say, therefore, that the song of the psalmist is not born of circumstances. No abiding song ever is.

Neither is he singing because he is possessed of a rugged determination. There are times that we sing from a sense of duty. We feel that for the sake of others it is the helpful thing to do, and in this we are right. There is something finely heroic about the man who refuses to parade his sorrow but rather locks it all in his heart and smiles on the world. It requires a high type of courage to keep a song upon the lips while there is a sob in the heart. Yet there are those big and brave enough for this taxing task. This was a practice that we urged with great enthusiasm during the stressful days of World War I. We sang lustily, "Pack up your troubles in your old kit bag, and smile, smile, smile." And some of us did it, though the smile sometimes changed into a grimace the moment we were alone.

What, then, is the source of his song? It is a gift of God. "He hath put a new song in my mouth," declares this poet joyously. Then his song has a fountain source that is abiding. His music need never be hushed into silence nor changed into discord. On the farm where I lived as a boy there is one of the loveliest springs that ever sang its way out of the hills. We call it the Basin Spring. "The trees fold their green arms around it, trees a century old, and the winds go whispering through them and the sunbeams drop their gold." The waters of this spring used to flow over a large flat rock. But one day hands that have probably been dust for centuries chiseled a basin upon the face of this rock. That basin, even in times of severest drought, is always filled to overflowing because it has water constantly flowing into it from an unfailing reservoir among the great hills. And so it is with the music of this joyous singer. His song is born of the inexhaustible resources that are locked in the heart of God.

2. The Nature of This Poet's Song

What is the nature of this poet's song?

His is a song of deliverance. "He brought me up also out of an horrible pit, out of the miry clay." How he ever got into this pit we are not told. He may have plunged into it through some great and devastating calamity. He may have fallen into it through his own willfulness or carelessness or spiritual stupidity. But regardless of how he had come to be there, there he was, and there was no shutting his eyes to his tragic situation. He could never forget the stark horror of it all. The place was dark and cold. It was unspeakably lonely and as silent as death itself. And that which brought his awful plight to the very climax of hopelessness and despair was that he could find no solid resting place for his feet. For this pit did not have firm masonry for its floor. It did not even have water. It only had stenchful mire that gripped him with tenacious fingers and slowly dragged him into a ghastly grave.

It is Victor Hugo, I think, who tells the story of a man caught in the quicksand. One moment this man is walking in safety. Then his path begins to cling to his feet a bit. A few more steps and he is bogged down to his knees. He then begins to struggle frantically. But the more he struggles, the deeper he sinks. Soon the treacherous sand has reached his waist. By this time the unfortunate victim has become desperate. He now realizes that he is being slowly swallowed by a hideous, blind mouth that is absolutely without mercy. He cries for help, but there is no response. He looks at the clouds floating in the blue and the birds as they soar above his head, and they seem to mock him. He prays, he shrieks, he curses. He struggles with every ounce of his energy, but the implacable mouth still swallows him only the faster. At last his final wild wail ends in a gulp. The cruel sand has filled his mouth, and the futile struggle is over.

The singer tells us that he was like this man, that he, too, was sinking and was horribly sure that all was over, that he, too, cried desperately for help. But here he has a different story to tell. There was One who answered his cry. He stretched up a helpless hand, and that hand was seized by One who was mighty, and he felt himself lifted to safety. Since then he has had a song upon his lips. It is a song of deliverance. Some of us can join him in the singing of it, for such a song befits the lips of every person who has greatly sinned and who has been greatly saved. Such a song is even more fitting for the lips of those who, through being reared in Christian homes and through the guidance of Christian parents, have been spared the agony of falling into the horrible pit out of which this poet had to be rescued at exceedingly great cost both to himself and to his Lord.

Then this song of the poet is a song of security. "He (hath) set my feet upon a rock, and established my goings." This marvelously delivered man walks today with an assured confidence. His confidence, however, is not born of his faith in himself but of his faith in God. It is God who has enabled him to say with the prophet, "He maketh my feet like hinds' feet." God has given him a bracing sense of security. God has made it possible for him to sing with the author of the Twenty-third Psalm, "Yea, though I walk through the valley of the shadow of death, I will fear no evil." His footing is firm and secure. He does not look to tomorrow with feverish fear as he once did. The old horror is gone, and he can now look ahead with quiet eyes, knowing that the God who keeps him today will be sufficient for him tomorrow.

This song is also a song of gratitude. In the consciousness of the deliverance and security that God in His goodness had given him, he could not withhold his praise. He burst into song as naturally as the bird that "lets his illumined being o'errun with the deluge of summer it receives." We are not so grateful as we ought to be, any of us. One day Jesus healed ten lepers. Having been healed, nine of them hurried upon their separate ways, utterly forgetful of the Healer. Only one came back with a song of praise upon his lips. Too often we join the nine. Too rarely we join the one. The psalmist is among those who came back. His is a song of thanksgiving.

Finally, this song is winsomely and fascinatingly new. Its newness, however, is not born of the fact that this singer is saying something that has never been said before. It is not a bizarre song; it is a new song. I am glad that this is so. There is no real virtue in mere novelty. Neither new songs nor new gospels are needed, if by "new" we mean only the unusual and the novel. I recently heard a wise preacher say to a group of theological graduates: "My young friends, when you begin to preach and one comes forward at the close of the service to say to you, 'That was a new thought you gave me today, I never thought of that before,' don't be too elated over it. The chances are that he will never think of it again." This song is new, not because it is unusual, but because it is born of experiences that are new and vital to the singer.

Yesterday a hearse passed you on the street. You only gave it a brief glance. A hearse is such a common sight. Yet to some who followed, that journey to the cemetery was as new and poignant as if they were the first who had ever been called upon to bury their dead out of their sight. The other day I heard a young mother talking to her first baby. She was saying the same sweet, ungrammatical nothings that generations of mothers have said. Yet they were fascinatingly new and lovely. They were born of experience. And here is a man and a woman who have come to love each other. In their own ears how amazingly new and startling are the things they say. Yet they have been said over and over again countless millions of times. Recently a mother found an old letter that was so sentimental that she told her daughter frankly she was ashamed of her for writing such a letter. But when the daughter looked it over she found to her delight it was not her letter at all, but her mother's. Love talks the same language through the centuries, but it is always fascinatingly new.

Jesus said: "Every scribe which is instructed unto the kingdom of heaven is like unto a man that is an householder, which bringeth forth out of his treasure things new and old." That is what the psalmist is doing. That is what we can do. If we have a fresh, vital experience of God, our song will be as new and fresh as the first rose of June, yet as old as the ordered coming of the seasons. It will be as new as the first smile that dimples the cheek of the mother's first baby, yet it will be as old as motherhood. That was an old sky into which Shelley's skylark flew, but the bird looked at it as if his were the first eyes that had ever seen it, and as he looked he sang a song so new that the poet had to exclaim—

> Teach me half the gladness
> That thy brain must know,
> Such harmonious madness
> From my lips would flow,
> The world should listen then—
> As I am listening now.

Just so long as we are making new discoveries in God, so long will our song be enchantingly new.

3. The Good of This New Song and Why Should We Covet It

Now what is the good of this new song? Why should we covet it ourselves?

It is an unspeakable benediction to him who possesses it. Song means joy, laughter, gladness. Our present-day religion is a bit short on joy. Therefore it is short on power. "The joy of the Lord is your strength." It is a source of strength in our hours of bereavement. It is a source of strength when our dreams fail to come true. It is a steady staff upon which to lean when the rain is on the roof and the light has gone out of the skies. It is a strong anchor when the fierce tempest toys with our bark and "sorrow sits sobbing like a troubled ghost in every chamber of the heart."

Then it is a source of strength in our times of temptation. There are those who, in some measure, can resist the downward tug through sheer force of will. There are others who may be able to get past the death-haunted shores where the sirens sing by the poor expedient of stuffing wool into their ears. But the method of Ulysses was far better. He took on board with him one whose song was so much more winsome than that of the sirens that the music of those death-dealing creatures lost its spell. This is a sure way of victory for ourselves. The most luring songs that the world can sing will lose their spell and become mere jarring discord if we have singing in our hearts the new song of the psalmist.

This new song is not only a benediction to the singer, but to his fellows as well. "Many shall see it," sings our poet, "and fear, and shall trust in the Lord." "Many shall see it." Does not the poet use the wrong word? Should he not have said, "Many shall hear it"? Who sees a song? Yet so it is written. And you doubtless recall the wise conclusion that John Milton reached when, as a lad, he dreamed of writing a poem that the world would not willingly let die. He declared that he who would write a great poem must himself be a poem. And our singer has attained in some measure the high standard set by Milton. With this new song upon his lips that is but an echo of the song within his heart, he has himself become a song. There is a winsomeness and charm about his life that may be seen as well as heard. He is so in tune with the Infinite that those whose lives he touches cannot resist his spell. They yearn to know his secret, and, knowing it, they, too, come to trust in the Lord.

We who profess to be Christians are often dreadfully short on winsomeness. We read of some of the early saints that great grace was upon them; that is, they were gracious, fascinating, appealing. To associate with them was to become keen and eager to find what they had found. But when the Pharisee had finished thanking God that he was not as other men, I wonder who followed him home to ask him about the deep things of the soul. I wonder who went to him to inquire wistfully how they, too, might separate themselves from the unwashed crowd of "extortioners, unjust, adulterers" and become faultless and unstained like himself. I wonder what man came with eager step and with an impassioned appeal that would take no denial to learn how he might rise to the sublime height of fasting twice a week. You know, no man came. And it was not because this Pharisee was not religious. It was rather because he was horribly religious. He was not in tune with God, and there was no wooing harmony in his life.

Ole Bull, the famous Norwegian violinist, had a friend, Leif by name, who averred that he had no ear for music. The fact that the violin of his fellow countryman had an angel choir hidden within it mattered nothing to him. The fact that Ole Bull could change his bow into a magic wand and make tempests crash and thunder or birds sing or brooks leap and prattle as songfully as the laughter of a happy child did not interest Leif in the least. He even refused to go and hear Ole Bull play. But the great violinist won him in the end. How did he go about it? He did not crash his violin over his friend's head. He did not lecture him. He did not give him a scathing description of the man who is not moved by concord of sweet sounds. He went to where Leif was working and played for him—played with all the power of his compelling genius. And what was the result? It is easy to guess. Leif's heart became warm, his face softened, and his eyes grew big with tears. And then and there the soul of this scientist and inventor was taken captive by the charm of music.

It is even so that this singer of the new song seeks to take captive the hearts of human beings. He knows that we are not going to win the world by our wails. We are not going to win by our complaints. We are not going to win by persistently prating about what is wrong with the church. We are not going to win by proclaiming what a distressingly hard time we are having as we try to serve the Lord. We are not going to win by discordant lives that clash like violins played out of tune. But we can win through the appealing winsomeness of lives in tune with the Christ. If there is a harmony about our lives that the world cannot give and cannot take away, somebody is going to ask the secret. We are very short on inner music. We are sadly lacking in freshness and newness. If we show the way to the new song by the beauty and charm of our lives, "many shall see it, and fear, and shall trust in the Lord."

Singing to the Lord

William Culbertson (1905–1971) was born and educated in Philadelphia and was identified all of his ministry with the Reformed Episcopal Church of America. He pastored churches in Pennsylvania and New Jersey and in 1937 was elected Bishop of the New York and Philadelphia Synod. In 1942 he became Dean of Education at the Moody Bible Institute in Chicago and in 1947 was named acting president upon the death of Will H. Houghton. In 1948 he became president of the school, a position he held with distinction until 1971, when he was named Chancellor. "My first impression and the lasting one," said Dr. Wilbur M. Smith, "is that he is a man of God." He was in great demand as a preacher and widely recognized as a leader in Christian education.

This sermon comes from the compilation of his Moody Bible Institute "Founder's Week" messages, *The Faith Once Delivered*, published in 1972 by Moody Press, and is used by permission.

William Culbertson

2

SINGING TO THE LORD

Let the word of Christ dwell in you richly; in all wisdom teaching and admonishing one another with psalms and hymns and spiritual songs, singing with grace in your hearts unto God (Colossians 3:16).

YOU ARE AWARE that singing is one of the few earthly exercises which will be perpetuated in heaven. There are many things we do down here that will not be continued in heaven. It is wonderful to have the opportunity of witnessing to someone about the Lord Jesus in order to win him or her to Christ. But can you imagine going next door up in heaven and trying to win someone to Christ? Bless your heart, he wouldn't be there unless he had already been won.

It is wonderful to get under the burden of prayer for some one specific request, some circumstance of life. Perhaps someone is sick, or a missionary may be in a place of great trial where discouragement has gripped his or her heart, or someone may be confronted with enemies that have the power, humanly speaking, to take his very life. Word reaches us and we bow together and meet at the throne of grace and we pray in intercession. Well, in heaven there won't be such circumstances, there won't be such enemies.

But there is one thing we shall have the privilege of doing in heaven that we have the privilege of doing on earth, and that is to sing. We shall sing the song of Moses and of the Lamb.

1. The Prominence of Song in the Bible

Let us think together in a simple way about singing and about praising God in the Scriptures. You have noticed the prominence of song in the Bible. Someone has said that heathenism has no hymnbook. That is true. The heathen have their weird chants and their dirges of despair, but they have no joyful song. In striking contrast is the prominence of song in the Word of God.

There is the song of Miriam in Exodus 15. God had wrought for His people and opened the Red Sea before them. God had destroyed the enemies of Israel, and song was born in the heart of Miriam. She praised Jehovah, the God of Israel.

There is the song also of Deborah, because God had vouchsafed to Israel deliverance from the Caananites under the leadership of Barak. Sisera was dead and Jabin, the king of Caanan, was vanquished. In Judges 5, in a tremendous outburst of triumph, the victory song of Deborah is recorded for us.

There is the song of Moses, a little different in character, a little different in emphasis, found in Deuteronomy, beginning in the latter part of chapter 31 and continuing on through chapter 32. Bible teachers under whom I sat in my early days used to refer to it as the swan song of Moses, the word of praise and testimony to the faithfulness of God in which the resounding word of emphasis is upon God as the rock of His people. What a great song it is.

Of course I need not refer to the songs of David, the songs of Asaph, the songs of the sons of Korah and others who were used of God to give us the Psalter.

May I remind you that the Lord Jesus sang with the eleven men He had chosen out of the world before they left the upper room the night in which He was betrayed. It is recorded, "After they had sung a hymn they went out." I recognize what some of my brethren mean when they say they are glad they did not live in the time the Lord Jesus was on earth, because we have so many more blessings and we have His Spirit. But frankly, I would love to have been in that Upper Room to hear Him sing. I know what He sang. He sang the great *Hallel*, Psalms 116, 117 and 118. I would love to have heard Him sing it. But I am going to hear Him sing someday, because Zephaniah 3:17 says He is going to sing.

I remember Paul and Silas sang. They were in prison in Philippi, and at midnight they were giving their praise to God in song. I suggest that that is the genius of Christianity. Anybody can sing when he or she is happy; anybody can sing when circumstances are all right according to worldly standards, but it takes a Christian to sing at midnight in the prison.

You see, the Bible is a book of song, and someday, the full open *diapason* of heaven's music will be heard and a new song will be sung. We read of it in Revelation 5:9–10: "Worthy art thou to take the book, and to open the seals thereof: for thou wast slain, and didst purchase unto God with thy blood men of every tribe, and tongue, and people, and nation, and madest them to be unto our God a kingdom and priests; and they reign upon the earth."

It is interesting to note, as well, that hymnologists have found hymn fragments in the Bible. It has been suggested that there are verses which might well have been sung by congregations that met in the name of the Lord Jesus in the early days of the New Testament Church. "Awake, thou that sleepest, and arise from the dead, and Christ shall give thee light" (Eph. 5:14, KJV). Then that tremendous word of praise indicating who the Lord is and what He has done: God "was manifested in the flesh, justified in the spirit, seen of angels, preached among the nations, believed on in the world, received up in glory" (1 Tim. 3:16, ASV). It is the rhythmical formation of such words in the original language that lead hymnologists to believe that here and there are fragments of songs of the early church in the Book of God.

I suggest to you that it is not an accidental occurrence that so much place is given to song in the Bible. It was Augustine of Hippo who delighted to remind his hearers that a new salvation demands a new song. The Bible is a book of salvation; therefore it is a book of song.

2. Who Can Sing?

The second thing that I would suggest we think about is who can sing. I remember early in study of the Bible I came upon something. I was much more dogmatic about it then than I am now, but I still think there is a residuum of truth here that we ought not to pass by. Do you know there is not one place in all the Bible where the word angel is used as the subject of the verb *to sing.* Now, I know about the reference in Job concerning the morning stars singing together, and I am willing to say angels can sing. I take it that they could sing better than some of us. I remember it was said about Lucifer before the fall that "the workmanship of thy tabrets and of thy pipes was in thee," and I take that to mean his voice was beautiful, that it was like an organ with pipes. So I don't doubt angels can sing, but it is an interesting thing that Scripture always says that the angels *said.* Even when the *Gloria in Excelsis* was given to the shepherds in the fields of Bethlehem, we read that the angels *said,* "Glory to God in the highest, and on earth peace, good will toward men" (Luke 2:14, KJV). It is just an interesting observation that the Bible does not seem to make much of the singing of angels, though they may well sing and sing as beautifully as creatures could ever sing.

But the Bible talks about redeemed men and women singing. "Let the word of Christ dwell in you richly; in all wisdom teaching and admonishing one another with . . . songs." It is those in whose hearts the Word of God dwells who sing, and only those who know the Lord could be said to have the Word of God in their hearts. Actually, this Scripture suggests that the Word of Christ is at home in their hearts. It is not only that they have memorized some Scripture, but the Word of God is at home in them, because there is a correspondence between the way they live and the way the Word of God says they should live. The Word of Christ dwells in them. These are they that sing.

Notice the end of Colossians 3:16 makes this plain: "Singing with grace in your hearts to the Lord" (KJV). And who can have grace in their hearts except those who are God's children? We have received of the grace of God, grace upon grace, and we have been saved by grace through faith, "and that not of yourselves, it is the gift of God" (Eph 2:8). So Colossians 3:16 is saying to us that it is those who know the Lord, who know what the grace of God means in reaching lost sinners and saving them, those in whose hearts the Word of God dwells, who are exhorted in the Word of God to sing. The Word of Christ has found hospitality in our hearts, the grace of God has been received and accepted if we have responded to the gift of God's grace, and so we sing.

3. Why Do We Sing?

Another word—Why do we sing? First of all, we sing in praise to the Lord. What does the text say? "Singing unto God." For the Word is: "Teaching and admonishing one another with psalms and hymns and spiritual songs, singing with grace in your hearts unto God." Our hymns of praise, our hymns of worship are hymns of worship and praise to our God. This is a fitting way to come into the presence of the Lord, with praise on our lips as the reflection of the praise of our hearts.

I wonder if we remember this scripture when we sing our hymns of praise. There are hymns in which we are not singing to one another, and even though there were not another human ear to hear, it would make no difference; the hymn is a hymn of worship, of adoration, of praise. Look at just one of them with me. Take your hymnbook and put it right by your Bible. That is a good combination. You read the Word and let God speak to you; you pray to Him, and then it is wonderful to take a hymnbook and just read the hymns. This is a hymn of adoration, a hymn of worship and praise. It is an old hymn, which comes to us actually from the twelfth century, written by Bernard of Clairvaux.

> O Jesus, King most wonderful!
> Thou Conqueror renowned!
> Thou Sweetness most ineffable,
> In whom all joys are found!

You can pray that hymn. It gives expression to thoughts in my heart that somehow I haven't been able to find words to express. Listen to these stanzas:

> When once Thou visitest the heart,
> Then truth begins to shine,
> Then earthly vanities depart,
> Then kindles love divine.

And again:

> Thy wondrous mercies are untold,
> Through each returning day;
> Thy love exceeds a thousand-fold,
> Whatever we can say.

You see, alone before the Lord we can utter these words, for here is a hymn of worship and of praise to God. The first purpose of our song should be to praise the Lord.

But there are hymns that have other purposes. A hymn may be a testimony and a witness to someone who hears it and may even lead him or her to inquire about the faith.

We have already referred to Paul and Silas in jail. They were in the innermost prison, having been beaten, which means their backs were bloody. They were put in stocks, which means they were cramped and held in one position, their feet and hands being bound. Yet in that condition and in that place, which, of course, would have been a vermin-infested dungeon, they began to sing. What effect do you think that had on the jailer and on the prisoners? Those are very interesting words in Acts 16:25: "About midnight Paul and Silas were praying and singing hymns unto God, and the prisoners *were listening* to them." I hear a lot I do not like to hear, but when I listen to something, I am giving attention. I don't think I am reading anything extra into this verse when I say one of the prisoners may have said to another, "Listen to those men. We know what they went through. We have been beaten with stripes, we have been in a dungeon, we have been in stocks; but listen to those men. Either they are insane, or else they have something we don't have. I am going to hear what they have to say." How did the jailer know enough to come to Paul and Silas and ask, "What must I do to be saved?" Where did he ever get the word *saved*. Don't ask me to prove it, but I think he heard them singing about it. You see, a hymn or a song may be a testimony or a witness to others, to fellow Christians, or to the unsaved.

But it also may have as its purpose to build up Christian character and life. Did you notice that Colossians 3:16

speaks about "teaching and admonishing one another with psalms and hymns and spiritual songs"? In other words, there is a didactic purpose, teaching; there is an exhortation, an admonishing one another "with psalms, hymns and spiritual songs." In our use of "psalms, hymns, and spiritual songs," we should exhort one another.

There are hymns in which we teach one another. We can open our songbooks almost at random and find a teaching hymn. Look at the words of this hymn by Zinzendorf:

> Jesus, Thy blood and righteousness
> My beauty are, my glorious dress;
> Midst flaming worlds, in these arrayed,
> With joy shall I lift up my head.

What are we doing there? Reminding ourselves of the great truth that Christ died for us, and that the righteousness of God is ours through faith in the Lord Jesus. Therefore we can sing:

> Bold shall I stand in Thy great day,
> For who aught to my charge shall lay?
> Fully absolved from these I am,
> From sin and fear, from guilt and shame.

These hymns have a message, and the proper singing of them involves teaching and admonishing one another.

So I suggest hymns are used to praise God, to give witness to our experience with God, to develop Christian character and life in setting forth the teaching of the Word of God. Thank God, in this last area I have mentioned are the great hymns of comfort.

"Our Great Savior" is a favorite of mine. Dr. J. Wilbur Chapman develops this hymn around one by Charles Wesley. Notice these lines: "Jesus, Lover of my soul." Look at the next stanza: "Let me hide myself in Him." The next: "While the billows o'er me roll"; the next: "While the tempest still is high"; and the last: "More than all in Him I find." Dr. Chapman took those words from "Jesus, Lover of My Soul" and developed this beautiful hymn about the Lord Jesus.

> Jesus! what a Friend for sinners!
> Jesus! Lover of my soul;
> Friends may fail me, foes assail me,
> He, my Savior, makes me whole.

That ought to do something to you if you are a Christian. It ought to make you stand up and even face the devil in the power of the blood of Christ and the power of the Holy Spirit. These hymns are hymns that teach us. They are not just words that we sing and then forget. How important it is that we should teach and admonish one another with psalms and hymns and spiritual songs. You see, the saints of God can be instructed and challenged and comforted by Christian songs.

4. What Are We to Sing?

What are we to sing? This verse in Colossians is almost duplicated in Ephesians 5: 19, where we are told to sing psalms and hymns and spiritual songs. I recognize that diligent students of the Word of God have some question as to Paul's use of these three terms. Very early in the church the Psalter was used. The word *hymn* was used by the Greeks many years before the New Testament was written. It was used of a song which was addressed to a god. If it were addressed to a man, it was because he claimed to be a god, the emperor, for example. The early Christians had an abhorrence of this word evidently, because it is not found in any of the writings of the apostolic Fathers, presumably because of its heathen connotation. Paul, however, uses it in Colossians 3 and Ephesians 5. Certainly we know he was using it for praise to God, the God and Father of our Lord Jesus Christ, the true God.

So early in the church, a hymn came to be recognized as any sacred song that was addressed to God. Augustine said there had to be three things true of a hymn. It definitely had to be a song, it had to be praise, and it had to be praise to God. Whether that was true when Paul used the word, I cannot say, but I like this distinction. We can sing psalms; we can sing hymns, those songs addressed to God in praise, and then this third category, spiritual songs.

Certainly early in the history of the church these were songs of experience. Spiritual people sang spiritual songs. There were battle songs and harvest songs and festal songs and marriage songs, but these are *spiritual* songs. They have to do with the things of the Spirit, with the Word of God. Presumably one Christian is testifying to another Christian in a spiritual song, at least very early in the history of the church that was the meaning of this word.

Here is another matter that may interest you. The only word used for song in the book of the Revelation is this word, and transliterated into English it is our word *ode.* It is a spiritual song which indicates something of one's own experience in the things of God. "Blessed assurance, Jesus is mine! Oh, what a foretaste of glory divine" is an example. What are we doing? We are testifying of an experience with God, and the reality of it should give substance and sincerity and integrity to the song.

As I close, look again at Colossians 3:16: "Let the word of Christ dwell in you richly; in all wisdom teaching and admonishing one another with psalms and hymns and spiritual songs, singing with grace in your hearts unto God." I wonder how often you have sung that way in church? This is the scriptural teaching of how Christians ought to sing. Oh, that we begin to see that this matter of praise and of song is an integral part of Bible teaching. It is a great inestimable privilege that we can stand and praise our God and teach and admonish one another in the things of God, singing psalms and hymns and spiritual songs to the Lord. Though we may not be soloists, our voices together will create harmony and beauty as we lift our praise to God on high.

I plead for a return to a scriptural singing, for the praise and the honor and the glory of God. Let this forgotten exhortation be a remembered exhortation.

Hallelujah!

Amzi Clarence Dixon (1854–1925) was a Baptist preacher who ministered to several congregations in the south before becoming pastor of the Moody Memorial Church in Chicago (1906–1911). He left Chicago to pastor the famous Metropolitan Tabernacle in London, "Spurgeon's Tabernacle" (1911–1919). He died in 1925 while pastoring the University Baptist Church, Baltimore, Maryland. A close associate of Reuben A. Torrey, Dixon helped him edit *The Fundamentals*. Dixon was a popular preacher in both Britain and America.

This message is from *Through Night to Morning*, reprinted in 1969 by Baker Book House.

Amzi Clarence Dixon

3

HALLELUJAH!

Praise ye the Lord (Psalm 146:1).

THE WORD *hallelujah,* which is translated "Praise ye the Lord," occurs, as I have counted, twenty-four times in the Book of Psalms and four times in the nineteenth chapter of Revelation, making twenty-eight times altogether in the Bible. In the Psalms it is the Hallelujah of earth, and in Revelation it is the Hallelujah of heaven. It is a word which cannot be translated by one word into any other language and is, therefore, transferred. It is about the same in Greek, Latin, German, French, Italian, Dutch, and English. It looks as if all nations are practicing for the Hallelujah chorus of heaven.

There are six Hallelujahs. Let us pass them in review.

1. The Hallelujah of Nature

The first use of the word is at the close of Psalm 104. This Psalm is a fine poem on nature. It begins by calling on the soul to bless God and then ascribes to God the greatness, honor, and majesty which a study of nature suggests to a religious mind. The light is God's garment. The heaven is the canopy which He has spread, and the foundations of the ocean were laid by Him. He makes the clouds His chariot and rides upon the wings of the wind. The thunder is His voice. He makes the springs which water bird and beast. The grass for the cattle, the trees for the nesting birds, the hills for the wild goats and the rocks for the conies are the expressions of His love and wisdom. He made the laws which govern the sun and moon. Even the darkness serves a benevolent purpose. In the midst of this beautiful scene man "goeth forth to his labor until the evening."

31

Then the psalmist poet turns to the ocean, "this great and wide sea, wherein are things creeping innumerable," with the ships on its surface and the monsters playing in its depths. God gives life and sustenance to all these.

The study of nature fills the psalmist with praise to God. He says, "My meditation of Him shall be sweet. I will be glad in the Lord." There is no conflict between the two books God has written for us, the book of Nature and the book of Revelation. God reveals Himself in both. The naturalist who does not see God in His works simply shuts his eyes and refuses to see. An agnostic is one who chooses blindness rather than sight. Everything in earth and sea and sky proclaims God. Over the door of the great museum of McGill University in Montreal Sir William Dawson wrote the twenty-fourth verse of this Psalm, "O Lord, how manifold are thy works: In wisdom hast Thou made them all." Sir William was a scientist, but he did not allow scientific prejudice to blind the eyes of his soul.

2. The Hallelujah of Providence

Psalm 105, which also closes with "Hallelujah," deals with the history of Israel, and the psalmist sees the footprints of God in history as well as in nature. It was God who covenanted with Abraham, "made oath unto Isaac," and "confirmed the same to Jacob." It was God who protected His people when they "were but few in number." It was God who "called for a famine upon the land" when prosperity had caused them to forget His laws. It was God who sent Joseph into Egypt and then Moses as the deliverer of His people. It was God who sent the darkness and turned their water into blood. It was God who spread a cloud over them for a covering and gave them "fire to give light in the night." It was God who "opened the rock" and quenched their thirst. The psalmist closes this review of God's providential dealings with a "Hallelujah."

With some it is easier to see God in nature than in providence. Jacob could praise God for grass and trees and stars, but when Joseph was taken he said, "All these things are against me." On another occasion the psalmist did not feel like praising, and he refused to shout "Hallelujah" with his lips when his heart did not prompt it. "Why art thou cast down, O my soul," he exclaims, "and why art thou disquieted within me? Hope thou in God; for I will yet praise Him." I do not feel like praising now, but I will hope for the time to come when I will praise Him. Indeed I will praise God that I will yet praise Him.

There is no kind of experience in which a Christian has a right to refuse to praise God, for "all things work together for good to them that love God." Praise God in the dark, for He makes the light to shine out of darkness. Praise God for sorrow, for Jesus said, "Your sorrow shall be turned into joy." Praise God for clouds, for it is upon the clouds that God shows His rainbow of love. Praise God for the furnace, for it is in the fire that the Son of Man delights to walk with you, and when you come out you will find that only your bonds have been burned. He who obeys the command, "Rejoice in the Lord," has a Hallelujah in his soul every minute of the day and night.

3. The Hallelujah of Grace

Psalm 106 begins and closes with "Hallelujah," and the key-note of its contents is in the first verse, "Give thanks unto the Lord, for His mercy endureth forever." He prays, "O visit me with Thy salvation," and he makes confession of sin: "We have sinned with our fathers; we have committed iniquity, we have done wickedly." Then follows a recounting of God's merciful dealings with His people in spite of their sins. "He remembered for them His covenant and repented according to the multitude of His mercies."

The saved sinner can sing this Hallelujah of mercy more loudly and sweetly than any other. And God's mercy fills him with song because His justice has been satisfied in Jesus Christ. Mercy can now rejoice against judgment because judgment has been met and mercy made possible through the atoning sacrifice of Christ. "Hallelujah for the cross" is the song of the redeemed. It comes to us from heaven and will return with us to heaven.

4. The Hallelujah of Praise

The Hallelujahs of nature, providence, and grace continue to the end, but the works of God recede while God Himself is more clearly seen. After "Hallelujah" in Psalm 111 come the words, "I will praise the Lord with my whole heart." After "Hallelujah" in Psalm 112: "Blessed is the man that feareth the Lord." After "Hallelujah" in Psalm 113: "Praise, O ye servants of the Lord, praise the name of the Lord." And as the Hallelujahs increase toward the end of the book, God alone is the object of praise. In Psalm 146, "Hallelujah, Praise the Lord, O my soul." In Psalm 147: "Hallelujah, for it is good to sing praises unto our God." In Psalm 148: "Hallelujah, Praise ye the Lord from the heavens." And the psalmist calls the roll of the Hallelujah choir consisting of angels, sun, moon, and stars, the heavens, "the dragons and all deeps," fire and hail, snow and vapors, strong wind, mountain and hills, trees, beasts and cattle, creeping things and flying fowl, men and women, old men and children. "Let them praise the name of the Lord, for His name alone is excellent."

In Psalm 149: "Hallelujah: Sing unto the Lord a new song," as if thought and words were failing him to express his praise to God. And the climax comes in the last verse of the last Psalm, "Let everything that hath breath praise the Lord. Hallelujah." God is greater and more worthy of praise than are His works in nature, providence, and grace.

5. The Hallelujah of Judgment

This appears in Revelation 19:1–2, "Hallelujah. Salvation and honor and power unto the Lord our God, for true and righteous are His judgments; for He hath judged the great harlot, which did corrupt the earth with her fornication. And again they said Hallelujah. And her smoke rose up forever and ever." The Hallelujah of judgment seems to shock sentimental natures who cannot endure the thought that God could allow anyone to go to hell. And yet anyone with a spark of nobility of character must rejoice over the apprehension and punishment of certain criminals. When the papers published the fact that a young man entered a large room in Buffalo, New York, and stood in line with those who were receiving the greetings of President McKinley, that he might murder the man who was ready to greet him with kindness, some theologians in New England, who had been preaching that there was no hell, were frank enough to confess that there ought to be a hell for at least one man, for McKinley and his murderer ought not to be together in the same place. For such men to escape hell, unless they repent, would be cause for everlasting regret. The smoke of their torment satisfies the sense of justice which every righteous soul has. For them to escape punishment would make a discordant note in God's universe. The Hallelujah of judgment is the response of noble natures to the justice of the retribution which comes upon those who wreck the character and destroy the happiness of others.

6. The Hallelujah of Sovereignty

"Hallelujah, for the Lord our God reigneth" (Rev. 19:6).

> Truth forever on the scaffold,
> wrong forever on the throne,
> Yet the scaffold sways the future,
> and behind the dim unknown
> Standeth God within the shadow,
> keeping watch above His own.

God seems to be dethroned, but He is not. The fact that He does not strike dead monsters of iniquity in human shape is proof that He is merciful. When, therefore, I read in the press of the orgies of those who lie in wait for the innocent and seek their destruction, I say, "Hallelujah! God is merciful." And when I read that some monster has been overtaken by retribution, I say with equal emphasis, "Hallelujah, God is just." When I hear a blasphemer revile God and the Bible, I say, "Hallelujah, God is merciful or he would be smitten dumb"; and when I hear the same man, yet not the same, because he has been transformed by grace, praising God for redemption through the blood of Christ, I say, "Hallelujah! Hallelujah, for the Lord God Omnipotent reigneth."

The Singers by the Sea

Alexander Maclaren (1826–1910) was one of Great Britain's most famous preachers. While pastoring the Union Chapel, Manchester (1858–1903), he became known as "the prince of expository preachers." Rarely active in denominational or civic affairs, Maclaren invested his time in studying the Word in the original and sharing its truths with others in sermons that are still models of effective expository preaching. He published a number of books of sermons and climaxed his ministry by publishing his monumental *Expositions of Holy Scripture*.

This message is taken from *The Best of Alexander Maclaren*, edited by Gains Glenn Atkins and published by Harper and Brothers in 1949.

Alexander Maclaren

4

THE SINGERS BY THE SEA

And I saw as it were a sea of glass mingled with fire: and
them that had gotten the victory over the beast, and over
his image, and over his mark, and over the number of his
name, stand on the sea of glass, having the harps of God.
And they sing the song of Moses the servant of God, and
the song of the lamb (Revelation 15:2–3).

THIS VISION OWES its form partly to the circumstances of the
seer and partly to an Old Testament reference. As to the
former, John's exile in Patmos occasions unusually numerous
allusions to the sea in this Book of the Revelation. The voice of
the glorified Redeemer, for instance, reminds him of the
thunder of the waves on the rocky coast. The mysterious
Beast rises from the sea's abysses, which might hide so much
that was foul and strange. Babylon sinks in ruin, like a
millstone tossed by an angel's hand into the sea. And when
the vision of the new heavens and the new earth dawns, one
of its characteristics is, "there shall be no more sea," that
emblem of estrangement, of rebellious power, of futile effort.

Similarly in this vision, the glassy sea shot with fire is
but a photograph of what was often seen from John's
rocky islet on some still morning when the sunrise "came
blushing o'er the sea," or on some evening when the wind
dropped and the flaming west dyed the watery plain with
a fading splendor.

Then, as to the other element which colors the represen-
tation here, we cannot fail to see that there is an allusion
to the Song of Miriam, sung on the banks of the Red Sea,
when Pharaoh and his host were buried in the mighty
waters. There, as here, the singers stand on the safe shore;
there, as here, they hymn a destruction which opened the
way to emancipation and joy. The allusion is underlined,
as it were, in the declaration that the Song which here is
sung is "the Song of Moses . . . and of the Lamb."

Now, of course, we cannot use highly imaginative representations, like that of my text, as if they were dogmatic statements, and we have to be very careful in deducing any inferences from such figurative language as this. But still, making all allowance for that, we may gather lessons that may be of use to us. We have here brought before us the victorious choir, their place by the glassy sea, and their triumphant song.

1. The Victorious Choir

The description of these jubilant singers is very striking. "They that had gotten the victory over," or, as the original is presented in the Revised Version, "they that had come victorious from"—and it would have been even better to have *out of* than *from*—"the beast, and his image and his mark, and the number of his name." They were conquerors who had fought their way out of a certain tyrannical dominion and had emerged into freedom. Now, I shall not spend time in the discussions which have been very fascinating to many people and do not seem to me to have been of much use to anybody, as to whether this "Beast" represents a person, and if so whether it is Nero, or whether it is some unknown and still future individual embodiment of certain tendencies. Never mind about that. The important question is, what made the Beast a beast?

Well—bestiality, to begin with, which, being turned into modern English, is sensuous animalism. Man is poised in the midst between two orders of being—if I may use the word *order* in reference to one of them—and he may rise or he may sink. He may go up to the level of divinity; he may come down to the level of bestiality. And if he does not do the one, he will do the other. You have only to look around you today to see the animal beneath a great deal of the veneer of civilization and refinement in modern society. The unblushing sensuality, or if I may not use that word, I may at least say sensuousness, of many modern ideals in art, in literature, in daily life—what is it but the beast in the man coming to be predominant? How much that is unblushingly practiced, and even defended and applauded, is really giving a free hand to the sensuous, which ought never to get a free hand, letting the mutineers come up on deck and take command of helm and sextant, or flinging the reins on the neck of the steeds, which do noble work when they are well held in, but set the heavens on fire, like Phaeton's team, when they are allowed their way. There are other aspects of what makes the Beast a beast. I put them all in two phrases, God-forgetting selfishness and God-defying opposition of will against Christ. If you take the context you will find, amidst a great deal that is very difficult to understand, this one thing emphasized, that the Beast and the Lamb divide the world between them and that whoever is not on the side of the one is on the side of the other. Under which King? Who is *your* Lord and Master? You young people especially, are you going to serve the flesh, or are you going to put your heel on the neck of the brute and live for the God whom you may bring to dwell within you? Which are you doing?

The next point is that the dominion of this Beast, which is shorthand for all the lower and animal tendencies, is an established fact out of which a person has to fight his or her way. "They have gotten the victory *out of* the beast . . . and the number of his name." There is nothing in this world worth the having and the being, which is not the result of a deadly earnest fight. If you make up your minds, or if without ever having had the courage to make them up, you let yourselves drift into the position of taking up the line of least resistance and doing what is easiest, then your fate is settled, and down you will go. I do not mean in regard to outward things. You may prosper in them and win wealth or fame if your aims go in that direction; but in regard to the true aims of life, unless you are prepared to fight, you will be a poor creature while you live, and a wreck altogether when you come to die. They "got the victory out of the beast", plucked it from the very jaws of the brute; and that is what we have to do. As the good old-fashioned hymn says:

> Now we must fight if we would reign;
> Increase our courage, Lord.

But there is one more thing to note about these victorious choristers. How did they get the victory? There is only one answer to that question—because they joined themselves to the Victor-Lamb. It is a strange paradox that runs through this Book of the Revelation, that, as I have already suggested, the Lamb is pitted against the Beast; and with entire destruction of the verisimilitude of the metaphor, the Lamb is made to be a Warrior-Lamb, Who "goes forth"—strange as it sounds—"conquering, and to conquer." That covers a deep truth. Christ cures the animalism of humanity by His sacrifice on the Cross and by His meekness and gentleness. And if you are ever to overcome your worst self and to have any share in that jubilant song of triumph at the last, I believe in my heart of hearts that the only way by which you can do so is by trusting yourself to Him who "teaches our hands to war and our fingers to fight."

When He said to us, "be of good cheer; I have overcome the world," He implied that "this is the victory that"—for us—"overcometh the world, even our faith," by which we unite ourselves with Him, participating by derivation in His victorious power, and, therefore, are "more than conquerors through him that loved us." They have "gotten the victory from the beast." Let me beseech you to fight under the same Leader and with the same weapons as they did, or the Beast will gain dominion over you.

And now turn to the second point—

2. The Glassy Sea by Which the Victors Stood

Of course, the allusion to the story in Exodus and the propriety of the picture make it necessary that we should suppose that they who stand "on the sea of glass" are not represented as if they had their feet planted on its calm surface, but that *on* here means "above," "by the side of," on the safe shore, with the glassy sea stretching in front of them. Now this sea of glass, by which these victors stood, has appeared already in this book, where it is represented as lying placid and even before the Divine Throne. I suppose that both there and in our text, it represents by a very natural metaphor the aggregate of the Divine dealings and self-manifestations to men, on whose calm surface, if I may so say, as on a great, shining mirror, the throne of God and He who sits upon it are in some degree reflected. One of the psalms has the same idea, in a somewhat different form, when it says, "Thy way is in the sea, and thy path in the deep waters, and thy footsteps are not known." Another psalm echoes the thought when it says, "Thy judgments are a mighty deep." And one of the apostles winds up his discussion about the mysteries of the kingdom of God with, "Oh! the depth of the riches of the wisdom and knowledge of God. How unsearchable are His judgments." So I suppose we may consider that it is in accordance with the analogy of Scripture, as well as with the natural propriety of the symbolism, if we see in this sea of glass mingled with fire an emblem of the whole dealings of God with humanity, through which are ever and anon shot, as it were, fiery streaks like the scarlet threads in Venetian glass.

This noble symbol carries with it some great and precious thoughts. That sea is transparent. It is deep, but it is not dark by reason of mud but by reason of its clear translucent depth; and when vision fails, it is not because of obscuration there but because of our weak sight. I have seen a like sea, without a speck of mire or dirt and with no weed on its margin, rising and falling on marble cliffs that it had polished into discovery of their golden veins. Such is this "glassy sea," pure and clean. "The judgments of the Lord are true and righteous altogether." We know their motives and purposes; they come from Love; they tend toward man's perfecting. And if at any time it is difficult to hold fast by that belief as to their origin because of their complexity or difficult to see how they tend to that issue, still, as does the psalm to which I have already referred, we have to link together the two conceptions: "Thy way is in the sea" and "Thy way is in the sanctuary."

Again, the sea of glass was calm and stable. To us, tossing upon it, it often looks tempestuous enough. To them, looking down from above, it is smoothed into a watery plain, a glassy mirror. That crystal sea was shot with fire. The judgments of God necessarily are sometimes punitive, retributive, destructive, but they that are in sympathy with the Lamb and have shaken off the tyranny of the Beast, in the measure in which they have done so, even here and now see in them and understand "the loving-kindness of the Lord" even when He smites.

And so I come to the last point—

3. The Song of This Victorious Choir

I do not attempt to expound it. I simply wish to draw attention to its central thought. These conquering choristers stand like Miriam and her maiden band with their timbrels on the safe shore, and as they look out on the calm waters that have buried Pharaoh and his hosts, they lift up their song of praise because of the destructive judgments that have led to liberty. The gist of their song is this, that God's dealings with humanity—the transparent crystal and the fiery streaks—alike are the outcome of His righteous love and alike are intended to lead people to know and worship Him. Even when there come "terrible things in righteousness" to the world or to us individually, if we are wedded to Jesus Christ they will yield to us here, and far more clearly and continuously hereafter, occasions for thankfulness, for praise, for clear perception of the Divine character, and for more lowly worship at His feet. "When the wicked perish there is shouting," says Proverbs. And when God, as is sometimes the case, comes forth and smites into dust some hoary institution that has been the source of miseries to mankind, then people ought to rejoice and in spite of sympathy and compassion ought to feel that God has done a mighty thing in mercy, though mercy had an envelope of wrath. There is nothing of the weak sentimentality which characterizes some people's theories in the New Testament conception of God. He is the God of love, but His very love must sometimes nerve His arm to strike and sharpen His spear to slay.

Let us remember that that is true about our individual lives. Let us take our places where the choristers stand by the glassy sea, in so far as we can do so here and now. Let us recognize habitually that even the retributive and destructive and afflictive acts of God come forth from His righteousness and for our good, and we shall be less astonished when the bitter draught comes to our lips and be able to say, even while we take it: "The cup which my Father hath given me, shall I not drink it?" And afterward we shall stand like the harpers by the glassy sea and praise Him for our sorrows, our losses, our pains, and for all the way by which the Lord our God has led us.

So let us acquiesce in present imperfect knowledge and not be in too great a hurry to pronounce, with our fallible judgments and our partial information as to a half-finished process, what is in accordance with and what is contrary to the Divine nature. Abraham had the boldness to say: "Shall not the Judge of all the earth do right?"—which did not mean "I will acquiesce in His acts, though I cannot see their righteousness, because He did them"; but did mean: "People have a standard of right and wrong to which they expect that the Divine acts will conform." That is true, no doubt, but it is a principle that has to be very cautiously applied, for the reasons just stated. We see but a small segment of the circle here, and our judgment of it had best be suspended till we see the perfect round. We shall be most modest and wise if we "judge nothing before the time." But we can confidently accept Christ's promise: "What thou knowest not now; thou shalt know hereafter." Since we may hope to join the victorious choristers by the sea of glass, let us not contradict our future song of praise by our present murmurings and complaints.

Brethren, this vision shows us, too, the path of victory. Take Jesus Christ for your captain, and in His strength fight, and He will bring you at last to the eternal shore; and as the unsetting sun rises, it will touch with golden beams the calm ocean, beneath which the oppressors lie buried forever. If we let the Beast write his name on our foreheads, we shall sink with him in the mighty waters. If we take the Lamb first for our sacrifice and then for our King, He will break the yoke of bondage from off our necks and bring us at last to the safe beach and put a new song into our mouths of praise to Him who has gotten us the victory "over the beast . . . and the number of his name."

Praise, One of the Chief Employments of Heaven

Jonathan Edwards (1703–1758) was a Congregational preacher, a theologian, and a philosopher, possessing one of the greatest minds ever produced on the American continent. He graduated with highest honors from Yale in 1720 and in 1726 was ordained and served as co-pastor with his grandfather, Solomon Stoddard, in Northfield, Massachusetts. When Stoddard died in 1729, Edwards became sole pastor, a position he held until doctrinal disagreements with the church led to his resignation in 1750. He played a key role in The Great Awakening (1734–44) and is perhaps best known for his sermon "Sinners in the Hands of an Angry God."

This sermon is taken from *The Works of Jonathan Edwards*, Volume 2, published by Banner of Truth Trust in 1976.

Jonathan Edwards

5

PRAISE, ONE OF THE CHIEF EMPLOYMENTS OF HEAVEN

And I heard a voice from heaven, as the voice of many waters, and as the voice of a great thunder; and I heard the voice of harpers harping with their harps (Revelation 14:2).

WE MAY OBSERVE in these words:

Introduction

1. What it was that John heard, that is, the voice and melody of a company praising God. It is said in the next verse that they sung a new song before the throne.

2. Whence he heard this voice: "I heard," says he, "a voice from heaven." This company that he heard praising God was in heaven. It is said in the following verse, "They sung this song before the throne, and before the four living creatures, and the elders." But the throne of God and the four living creatures and the four and twenty elders, are all represented in these visions of John as being in heaven. So that this voice was the voice of the heavenly inhabitants, the voice of the blessed and glorious company that is in heaven before the throne of God there.

3. The kind of voice which is here set forth in a very lively and elegant manner; it is said to be as the voice of many waters and as the voice of mighty thunders and as the voice of harpers harping with their harps. Hereby several things are represented in a very striking manner.

The distance of the voice.

That it was the voice of a vast and innumerable multitude: so that it was as the voice of many waters. How naturally does this represent the joint, continual, and loud voice of a vast multitude at a distance, that it resembled the voice of many waters.

The loudness of the voice. It was as the voice of many waters and as the voice of a great thunder; which describes the extraordinary fervency of their praises and how lively and vigorous they were therein and how that everyone praised God with all his might. They all, joining together, sung with such fervency that heaven did as it were ring with their praises. The noise of thunder and the roaring of many waters are the most great and majestic sounds ever heard upon earth and are often spoken of in the Scriptures as the mightiest sounds. John could not distinctly hear what they said, but they being in heaven, at a great distance, he knew not what better to compare it to than to the roaring of the sea or a great thunder. Yet,

It was a melodious sound, signified by this expression, "I heard the voice of harpers harping with their harps." The harp was a stringed instrument that David made much use of in praising God. John represents the matter thus to us, that the voice which he heard, being at a great distance, was indistinct; and being of such a vast multitude, and such a mighty fervent voice that it seemed in some measure like distant thunder or the roaring of water, and yet he could perceive the music of the voice at the same time; though it was in some respects as thunder and the noise of water, yet there was a sweet and excellent melody in it. In short, though these comparisons of which John makes use to signify to us what kind of a voice and sound it was that he heard are exceedingly lively and elegant, yet this seems to be evident from them, that what he heard was inexpressible and that he could find nothing that could perfectly represent it. That a voice should be as the voice of many waters and as the voice of a great thunder and yet like the voice of harpers is to us not easily to be conceived of. But the case was that John could find no earthly sound that was sufficient to represent it; and therefore such various and different similitudes are aggregated and cast together to represent it. But thus much seems to be signified by it, that it seemed to be the voice of an innumerable multitude and that they were exceedingly fervent and mighty in their praises; that the voice of this multitude was very great and exceedingly full of majesty, and yet a most sweet and melodious voice at the same time.

Main Text

Doctrine: The work of the saints in heaven does very much consist in praising God.

1. *Proposition*: The Saints in Heaven Are Employed

They are not idle; they have there much to do; they have a work before them that will fill up eternity.

We are not to suppose when the saints have finished their course and done the works appointed them here in this world and are got to their journey's end, to their Father's house, that they will have nothing to do. It is true, the saints when they get to heaven rest from their labors and their works follow them. Heaven is not a place of labor and travail, but a place of rest. "There remaineth a rest for the people of God" (Heb. 4:9). And it is a place of the reward of labor. But yet the rest of heaven does not consist in idleness and a cessation of all action, but only a cessation from all the trouble and toil and tediousness of action. The most perfect rest is consistent with being continually employed. So it is in heaven. Though the saints are exceedingly full of action, yet their activity is perfectly free from all labor or weariness or unpleasantness. They shall rest from their work, that is, from all work of labor and self-denial and grief, care, and watchfulness, but they will not cease from action. The saints in glory are represented as employed in serving God, as well as the saints on earth, though it be without any difficulty or opposition. "And there shall be no more curse: but the throne of God and of the Lamb shall be in it; and his servants shall serve him" (Rev. 22:3). Yea, we are told that they shall serve God day and night, that is, continually or without ceasing: "Therefore are they before the throne of God, and serve him day and night in his temple" (Rev. 7:15). And yet this shall be without any manner of trouble, as it follows in the next verse: "They shall hunger no more, neither thirst any more, neither shall the sun light on them nor any heat" (v. 16). In this world saints labor, as it were, in the wearisome heat of the sun; but there, though they shall still serve God, yet shall the sun not light on them nor any heat. In one sense, the saints and angels in heaven rest not day nor night (Rev. 4:8); that is, they never cease from their blessed employment. Perfection of happiness does not consist in idleness, but on the contrary, it very much consists in action. The angels are blessed spirits, and yet they are exceedingly active in serving God. They are as a flame of fire, which is the most active thing that we see in this world. God Himself enjoys infinite happiness and perfect bliss, and yet He is not inactive but is Himself in His own nature a perfect act and is continually at work in bringing to pass His own purposes and ends. That principle of holiness that is in its perfection in the saints in heaven is a most active principle; so that though they enjoy perfect rest, yet they are a great deal more active than they were when in this world. In this world they were exceedingly dull and heavy and inactive, but now they are a flame of fire. The saints in heaven are not merely passive in their happiness. They do not merely enjoy God passively, but in an active manner. They are not only acted upon by God, but they mutually act toward Him, and in this action and reaction consists the heavenly happiness.

2. *Proposition*: Their Employment Consists Very Much in Praising God.

John the beloved disciple had often visions of heaven and in almost every instance had a vision of the inhabitants as praising God. So in the fourth chapter he tells us that he looked, and behold, a door was opened in heaven, and he was called up thither, and that he saw the throne of God and Him that sat on the throne; and there he gives us an account how those that were round about the throne were praising God; the four living creatures rest not day nor night, saying, Holy, holy, holy Lord God Almighty, which was, and is, and is to come. And when those living creatures give glory and honor and thanks to Him, the four and twenty elders fall down before Him and worship Him. Again in the fifth chapter, we have an account how they sing praises to Christ (vv. 8–9ff). There are also examples in 7:9–12; 11:16–17; 12:10; and in 15:2–4. And in the beginning of the nineteenth chapter we have an account how the hosts of heaven sing hallelujahs to God. By all which it most evidently appears that their work very much consists in praising God and Christ. We have but a very imperfect knowledge of the future state of blessedness, and of their employment; without doubt they have various employments there. We cannot reasonably question but they are employed in contributing to each other's delight. They shall dwell together in society. They shall also probably be employed in contemplating on God, His glorious perfections, and glorious works, and so gaining knowledge in these things. And doubtless they will be employed many ways that we know nothing of; but this we may determine, that much of their employment consists in praising God, and that for the following reasons:

Because they there see God. This is a blessedness promised to the saints, that they shall see God (see Matt. 5:8). That they see God sufficiently shows the reason why they praise Him. They that see God cannot but praise Him. He is a Being of such glory and excellency that the sight of this excellency will necessarily influence them that behold it to praise Him. Such a glorious sight will awaken and rouse all the powers of the soul and will irresistibly impel them and draw them into acts of praise. Such a sight enlarges their souls and fills them with admiration and with an unspeakable exultation of spirit.

'Tis from the little that the saints have seen of God and know of Him in this world that they are excited to praise Him in the degree they do here. But here they see but as in a glass darkly; they have only now and then a little glimpse of God's excellency; but then they shall have the transcendent glory and divine excellency of God set in their immediate and full view. They shall dwell in His immediate glorious presence and shall see face to face (see 1 Cor. 13:12). Now the saints see the glory of God but by a reflected light, as we in the night see the light of the sun reflected from the moon; but in heaven they shall directly behold the Sun of righteousness and shall look full upon Him shining in all His glory. This being the case, it can be no otherwise but that they should very much employ themselves in praising God. When they behold the glorious power of God, they cannot but praise that power: when they see God's wisdom that is so wonderful and infinitely beyond all created wisdom, they cannot but continually praise that wisdom; when they view the infinitely pure and lovely holiness of God whereby the heavens themselves are not pure in comparison with Him, how can they avoid to praise that beauty of the divine nature with exalted hearts! When they see the infinite grace of God and see what a boundless ocean of mercy and love He is, how can they but celebrate that grace with the highest praise!

Because they will have another sense of the greatness of the fruits of God's mercy than we have here in this world. They will not only have a sight of the glorious attributes of God's goodness and mercy in their beatific vision of God, but they will be sensible of the exceeding greatness of the fruits of it; the greatness of the benefits that He has bestowed. They will have another sense of the greatness and manifoldness of the communications of His goodness to His creation in general. They will be more sensible how that God is the fountain of all good, the Father of lights, from whom proceeds every good and perfect gift. We do now but little consider, in comparison with what we should do, how full the world is of God's goodness, and how it appears in the sun, moon, and stars, and in the earth and seas with all their fullness, and wheresoever we turn our eyes, and how all ranks and orders of being from the highest angel to the lowest insect are dependent upon and maintained by the goodness of God. These the saints in heaven clearly see; they see how the universe is replenished with His goodness and how the communications of His goodness are incessantly issuing from God as from an ever-flowing fountain and are poured forth all around in vast profusion into every part of heaven and earth, as light is every moment diffused from the sun. We have but faint imperfect notions of these things, but the saints in heaven see them with perfect clearness.

They have another sense of the greatness of God's goodness to mankind and to the church and to them in particular, than any of us have. They have another sense of the greatness of God's goodness in the temporal mercies which God bestowed upon them while they were here in this world, though they know that spiritual mercies are infinitely greater. But especially they have an immensely greater sense how great a gift the gift of God's only-begotten Son is. They have another sense of the greatness and dignity of the person of Christ, and how great a thing it was for Him to become human, and how great a thing it was for Him to lay down His life and to endure the shameful and accursed death of the cross. They have another sense how great the benefits are that Christ has purchased for humanity, how great a mercy it is to have sin pardoned and to be delivered from the misery of hell. They have another sense how dreadful that misery is, for the damned are tormented in the presence of the holy angels and saints, and they see the smoke of their torment and have another sense what eternity is and so are proportionately more sensible how great a mercy it is to be delivered from that torment. They have another sense how great a fruit of God's grace it is to be the children of God and to have a right and title to eternal glory. They are sensible of the greatness of the benefits that Christ has purchased by their experience; for they are in possession of that blessedness and glory that He has purchased; they taste the sweetness of it; and therefore they are more sensible what cause they have to praise God for these things. The grace and goodness of God in the work of redemption appears so wonderful to them that their thoughts of it do excite them to the most ardent praise. When they take a view of the grace of God and of the love of Christ in redemption, they see that there is cause that they should exert the utmost of their capacities and spend an eternity in praising God and the Lamb. It is but a very little that we at best can conceive of the greatness of the benefits of redemption, and therefore we are but little affected by it, and our praises for it are low and dull things.

Because they will be perfect in humility. In order to a person's being rightly disposed to the work of praise, he must be an humble person. A proud person is for assuming all praise to himself and is not disposed to ascribe it to God. It is humility only that will enable us to say from the heart, "Not unto us, not unto us, O Lord, but unto thy name be the glory." The humble person admires the goodness and grace of God to him. He sees more how wonderful it is that God should take such notice of him and show such kindness to him that is so much below His notice. Now the saints in heaven have this grace of humility perfected in them. They do as much excel the saints on earth in humility as in other graces. Though they are so much above the saints on earth in holiness and in their exalted states, yet they are vastly more humble than the saints on earth be. They are as much lower in humility as they are higher in honor and happiness. And the reason of it is that they know more of God; they see more of His greatness and infinite highness and therefore are so much more sensible how wonderful it is that God should take so much notice of them, to have such communion with them and give them such a full enjoyment of Him. They are far more sensible what unworthy creatures they have been, that God should bestow such mercies upon them, than the saints on earth. They have a greater sight of the evil of sin. They see more what filthy vile creatures they were by nature, and how dreadfully they provoked God by actual sin, and how they have deserved God's hatred and wrath. The saints in heaven have as much greater a sense of their unworthiness in their natural state than the saints on earth, as they have a greater sense of God's glorious excellency, for it is the sight of God's excellency which gives them a sight of their own unworthiness. And therefore they do proportionally admire the love of God to them in giving Christ to die for them and the love of Christ in being willing to offer Himself for their sins, and of the wonderful mercy of God in their conversion and bestowing eternal life upon them. The humble sense the saints have of their own unworthiness does greatly engage and enlarge their hearts in praise to Him for His infinite mercy and grace.

Because their love to God and Christ will be perfect. Love is a principal ingredient in the grace of thankfulness. There is a counterfeit thankfulness in which there is no love. But there is love in exercise in all sincere thankfulness. And the greater any person's love is, the more will he be disposed to praise. Love will cause him to delight in the work. He that loves God proportionately seeks the glory of God and loves to give Him glory. Now the hearts of the saints in heaven are all, as it were, a pure flame of love. Love is the grace that never fails; whether there be prophecies, they shall fail, whether there be knowledge, it shall vanish away. Faith shall cease in vision and hope in fruition, but love never fails. The grace of love will be exalted to its greatest height and highest perfection in heaven; and love will vent itself in praise. Heaven will ring with praise, because it is full of love to God. This is the reason that great assembly, that innumerable host, praise God with such ardency that their praise is as the voice of many waters and as the mighty thunderings, because they are animated by so ardent, vigorous, and powerful a principle of Divine love.

Application

1. This Subject May Be Applied in the Way of *Instruction*

Hence we may learn the excellency of this work of praising God. That it is a most excellent employment appears because it is a heavenly employment. It is that work wherein the saints and angels are continually employed.

If we sincerely and frequently praise God, we shall therein be like the heavenly inhabitants and join with them.

That it is the work of heaven shows it to be the most honorable work. No employment can be a greater honor to a man than to praise God. It is the peculiar dignity of the nature of man and the very thing wherein his nature is exalted above things without reason and things without life, that he is made capable of actively glorifying his Creator. Other creatures do glorify God; the sun, moon,

and stars, and the earth and waters and all the trees of
the field, and grass and herbs and fishes and insects do
glorify God (see Ps. 19:1–6; Job 12:7–8). But herein is the
peculiar dignity of the nature of man, that he is capable of
glorifying Him as a cause, by counsel, understandingly
and voluntarily, which is a heavenly work.

*This doctrine may give us an idea of the glorious and
happy state of the saints in heaven.* It shows how joyfully
and gloriously they spend their time. Joy is a great
ingredient in praise. There is an exultation of spirit in
fervent praise. Praise is the most joyful work in the
world. And how joyful a society are they that join together,
so many thousands and millions of them, with one heart
and one soul to sing a new song before the throne, that
fill heaven with their glorious melody! How joyful they
are in their work appears in the text by their fervency in
it, so that their voices resounded as the voice of many
waters, as the voice of a great thunder. What ineffable
joy was there in those harpers whom John heard harping
with their harps!

This shows how different a state the saints are in
heaven from what they are in this world. Here much of
the work to which the saints are called consists in labor-
ing, in fighting, in toilsome traveling in a waste howling
wilderness, in mourning, and suffering, and in offering up
strong crying and tears. But there in heaven their work
continually is to lift up their joyful songs of praise.

This world is a valley of tears, a world filled with sighs
and groans. One is groaning under some bodily pain, another is mourning and lamenting over a dear departed
friend; another is crying out by reason of the arm of the
oppressor. But in heaven there is no mixture of such
sounds as these; there is nothing to be heard among them
but the sweet and glorious melody of God's praises. There
is a holy cheerfulness to be seen throughout that blessed
society. "And God shall wipe away all tears from their
eyes, and there shall be no more death, neither sorrow
nor crying" (Rev. 21:4). They shall never have anything
more to do with sighing and crying; but their eternal
work henceforward shall be praise.

This should make us long for heaven, where they spend their time so joyfully and gloriously. The saints especially have reason to be earnestly breathing after that happy state, where they may in so joyful a manner praise God.

This may put natural persons upon reflecting on their own state, that they have no part nor lot in this matter. You are alien from the commonwealth of Israel. You are not one of the people of God. You do not belong to their society, that are to spend their eternity after that joyful manner, which you have now heard. You have no right nor portion in heaven. If you hereafter come and offer yourself to be admitted into this blessed society in your present state; if you come and try to be admitted, you will be thrust out; you will be driven away. If you come and knock and cry to be admitted to the wedding, saying, *Lord, Lord, open unto us*, all will be to no purpose! You will hear no other word except *Depart!* You shall be shut out into outer darkness. You shall not be permitted to sing among the children but shall be driven out to howl among dogs. "Blessed are they that do his commandments, that they may have a right to the tree of life, and may enter in through the gates into the city; for without are dogs" (Rev. 22:14–15). You are in danger of spending eternity, not in joyfully singing praises, but in a quite contrary manner; in weeping, in wailing, and gnashing of teeth; and blaspheming God because of your pains and because of your plagues. You shall see others coming from the east and the west, and sitting down with Abraham and Isaac and Jacob in the kingdom of God, taking their places among that blessed, happy society, and joining their voices in their heavenly music. But you see your lot; you shall have other work to do. "Behold, my servants shall sing for joy of heart; but ye shall cry for sorrow of heart, and howl for vexation of spirit" (Isa. 65:14).

2. This Subject May Be Applied in the Way of *Exhortation.*

If it be so that praising God is very much the employment of heaven, hence let all be exhorted to the work and duty of praising God. The following considerations will

show why we should be stirred up by this doctrine to this
work.

Reasons for Praise

*Let it be considered that the church on earth is the same
society with those saints who are praising God in heaven.*
There is not one church of Christ in heaven and another
here upon earth. Though the one be sometimes called the
church triumphant and the other the church militant, yet
they are not indeed two churches. By the *church triumphant*
is meant the triumphant part of the church; and by the
church militant, the militant part of it, for there is but one
universal, or catholic, church. "My dove, my undefiled, is
but one" (Song 6:9). "The body is one, and hath many
members" (1 Cor. 12:12). The glorious assembly and the
saints on earth make but one family. "Of whom the whole
family in heaven and earth is named" (Eph. 3:15). Though
some are in heaven and some on earth in very different
circumstances, yet they are all united, for there is but *one
body, and one spirit, and one Lord Jesus Christ. One God
and Father of all, who is above all, and through all, and in
all.* God has in Christ united the inhabitants of heaven and
the holy inhabitants of this earth and has made them one.
"That in the dispensation of the fullness of time, he might
gather together in one all things in Christ, both which are
in heaven, and which are on earth, even in him" (Eph.
1:10). Heaven is at a great distance from the earth; it is
called a *far country* (Matt. 25:14). Yet the distance of place
does not separate them so as to make two societies. For
though the saints on earth, at present, are at a distance
from heaven, yet they belong there; that is their proper
home. The saints that are in this world are strangers here;
and therefore the apostle reproved the Christians in his
day for acting as though they belonged to this world. "Why,
as though living in the world, are ye subject to ordinances?"
(Col. 2:20).

Some of a people may be in their own land and some in
a strange land and yet be but one people. Some of a
family may be at home and some sojourning abroad and
yet be but one family. The saints on earth, though they be

not actually in heaven, yet have their inheritance in heaven and are traveling toward heaven and will arrive there in a little time. They are closely related to the saints in heaven; they are their brethren, being children of the same Father and fellow-heirs with Jesus Christ. In Ephesians 2:19 the saints on earth are said to be *fellow-citizens with the saints, and of the household of God*. And the apostle tells the Christian Hebrews that they were "come to mount Zion, and to the city of the living God, the heavenly Jerusalem, and to an innumerable company of angels, to the general assembly and church of the first-born, which are written in heaven, and to God the Judge of all, and to the spirits of just men made perfect" (Heb. 12:22–24). But how were they *come* to this heavenly city and this glorious assembly, when they were yet here on earth? They were come to them, ere they were brought and united to them in the same family. But this is what I would inculcate by all this, that the church of God on earth ought to be employed in the same work with the saints in heaven, because they are the same society; as they are but one family, have but one Father, one inheritance, so they should have but one work. The church on earth ought to join with the saints in heaven in their employment, as God has joined them in one society by His grace.

We profess to be of the visible people of Christ, to be Christians and not heathens, and so to belong to the universal church. We profess therefore to be of the same society and shall not walk answerably to our profession, unless we employ ourselves in the same work.

Let it be considered, that we all of us hope to spend an eternity with the saints in heaven and in the same work of praising God. There is, it may be, not one of us but who hopes to be a saint in heaven and there continually to sing praises to God and the Lamb; but how disagreeable will it be with such a hope to live in the neglect of praising God now! We ought now to begin that work which we intend shall be the work of another world; for this life is given us on purpose that therein we might prepare for a future life. The present state is a state of probation and preparation, a state of preparation for the enjoyments and employment of another, future, and eternal state; and no one is ever admitted to those enjoyments and employments, but those who are prepared for them here. If ever we would go to heaven, we must be fitted for heaven in this world; we must here have our souls molded and fashioned for that work and that happiness. Our souls must be formed for praise, and they must begin their work here. The beginnings of future things are in this world. The seed must be sown here; the foundation must be laid in this world. Here is laid the foundation of future misery and of future happiness. If it be not begun here, it never will be begun. If our hearts be not in some measure turned to praise in this world, we shall never do anything at the work hereafter. The light must dawn in this world, or the sun will never rise in the next. As we therefore all of us would be, and hope to be, of that blessed company which praise God in heaven, we should now inure ourselves to the work.

Let it be considered that those works of God's mercy for which the saints in heaven will chiefly praise Him have been wrought among us in this world.

The mercy and grace of God for which the saints in heaven will chiefly praise Him is His mercy exercised in the work of redemption, which work has been wrought out in this world. This love of God is the chief object of their admiration and what they chiefly contemplate, and that employs their most ardent praises.

The grace of Christ, about which their praises will be principally employed, is that He should so love sinful man as to undertake for him, to take upon Him man's nature, and lay down His life for him. We find that is the subject of their praises. "And when he had taken the book, the four living creatures, and the four and twenty elders, fell down before the Lamb, having every one of them harps, and golden vials full of odors, which are the prayers of saints; and they sang a new song, Thou art worthy, for thou hast redeemed us to God by thy blood" (Rev. 5:8–9).

They will chiefly praise God for these fruits of His mercy because these are the greatest fruits of it that ever have been, far greater than the glorifying of saints. The saints in heaven will praise God for bestowing glory upon them; but the actual bestowment of glory upon them, after it has been purchased by the blood of Christ, is in no measure so great a thing as the purchasing of it by His blood. For Christ, the eternal Son of God, to become human and to lay down His life was a far greater thing than the glorifying of all the saints that ever have been or ever will be glorified from the beginning of the world to the end of it. The giving of Christ to die comprehends all other mercies, for all other mercies are through this. The giving of Christ is a greater thing than the giving of all things else for the sake of the Christ. This evidently appears from Romans 8:32: "He who spared not his own Son, but delivered him up for us all, how shall he not with him also freely give us all things?" So that the work of redemption is that for which the saints in heaven do chiefly praise God. But this work has been wrought here among us in this world. "The Word was made flesh, and dwelt among us." The incarnation of Christ was a thing that was brought to pass in this world, and the sufferings and death of Christ were also accomplished on earth. Shall heaven be filled with praises for what was done on earth, and shall there be no praises on earth where it was done?

Let it be considered that if you praise God sincerely in this world, it will be a sign that you are really to be one of those that shall praise Him in heaven. If any man be found sincerely glorifying God, he will in due time be brought to them, as one who is fit to be of their company. Heaven is the appointed place of all sincere praisers of God; they are all to be gathered together there. And no man can sincerely praise God, unless he be one of those who are redeemed from among men, one that God has separated from the rest of the world and set apart for Himself.

Let it be considered that if we begin now to exercise ourselves in the work of heaven, it will be the way to have foretastes of the enjoyments of heaven. The business and the happiness go together. This will be the way to have your heart filled with spiritual joy and comfort. If you heartily praise God you shall rejoice in Him, and He will show you more of Himself, of His glory and love, that you may still have greater cause of praise.

Directions for Praise

I proceed to give some *directions* for the performance of this work.

1. Be directed, in order to your acceptably performing this duty, to repent of your sins and turn to God. If you have not a work of conversion wrought in you, you will do nothing to any purpose in this work of praise. An unconverted person never once sincerely or acceptably praises God. If you would do the work of the saints in heaven, you must be, not only in profession, but really, one of their society; for there are none else can do their work. As in the verse following the text: "And they sung as it were a new song, before the throne, and before the four living creatures, and the elders; and no man could learn that song, but the hundred and forty-four thousand, which were redeemed from the earth." A hundred and forty-four thousand is a mystical number for the church of God or the assembly of the saints or those that are redeemed from the earth. There are none can learn the song that they sing in heaven, but those of that number. It is beyond the reach of all natural human beings, let them be persons of ever so great abilities and sagacity. They never can learn that heavenly song, if they be not of that number. For it is only the sanctifying, saving instruction of the Spirit of God that can teach us that song.

2. Labor after more and more of those principles from whence the praise of the saints in heaven does arise. You have already heard that the saints in heaven do praise the Lord so fervently because they *see* Him; labor therefore that you, though you have not an immediate vision of God as they have, may yet have a clear spiritual sight of Him, and that you may know more of God and have frequent discoveries of Him made to you.

You have heard that the saints in heaven make praise so much their work because of *the great sense they have of the greatness and wonderfulness of the fruits of the Lord's goodness.* Labor therefore to get your minds more deeply impressed with such a sense.

The saints in glory are so much employed in praise, because they are perfect in *humility* and have so great a sense of the infinite distance between God and them. They have a great sense of their own unworthiness, that they are by nature unworthy of any of the mercy of God. Labor therefore that you may obtain more of a sense of your own littleness and vileness; that you may see more what you are, how ill you have deserved mercy at the hands of God, and how you are less than the least of all His mercies.

The hearts of the saints in heaven are all inflamed with divine *love* which continually influences them to praise God. Seek that this principle may abound in you, and then you likewise will delight in praising God. It will be a most sweet and pleasant employment to you.

3. Labor in your praises to praise God, so far as may be, in the same manner that the saints do in heaven. They praise Him *fervently*, with their whole hearts and with all their strength, as was represented in vision in John by the exceeding loudness of their praise. Labor therefore that you may not be cold and dull in your praises, but that you also may praise God fervently.

The saints in heaven praise God *humbly*. Let it also be your delight to abase yourselves, to exalt God and set Him upon the throne, and to lie at His footstool.

The saints in heaven praise God *unitedly*. They praise Him with one heart and one soul in a most firm union. Endeavor that you may thus praise God in union with His people, having your hearts knit to them in fervent love and charity, which will be a great help to your praising and glorifying God unitedly with them.

3. This Subject May Be Applied in the Way of *Reproof* to Those Who Neglect the *Singing* of God's Praises

Certainly, such a neglect is not consonant to the hope and expectation of spending an eternity in that work. It is an appointment of God, that we should not only praise in our prayers, but that we should *sing* His praises. It was a part of divine worship, not only under the Old Testament, but the New. Thus we read that Christ and His disciples sung praises together (see Matt. 26:30). So it is commanded in Ephesians 5:19: "Be ye filled with the Spirit, speaking to yourselves in psalms, and hymns, and spiritual songs, singing and making melody in your hearts to the Lord." And in Colossians 3:16: "Let the word of Christ dwell in you richly in all wisdom; teaching and admonishing one another in psalms, and hymns, and spiritual songs, singing with grace in your hearts to the Lord." And also in 1 Corinthians 14:15: "I will sing with the spirit, and I will sing with the understanding also." So also the saints in heaven are represented as singing God's praises. And is that their happy and glorious employment, and yet shall it be so neglected by us, who hope for heaven? If there be any of the godly that do neglect this duty, I would desire them to consider how discordant such a neglect is with their profession, with their state, and with the mercies which God has bestowed. How much cause has God given you to sing His praise! You have received more to prompt you to praise God than all the natural human beings in the world; and can you content yourself to live in the world without singing the praises of your heavenly Father and your glorious Redeemer?

Parents ought to be careful that their children are instructed in singing, that they may be capable of performing that part of divine worship. This we should do, as we would have our children trained up for heaven; for we all of us would have our children go to heaven.

4. This Subject May Be Applied in the Way of *Consolation* to the Godly

It may be matter of great comfort to you that you are to spend your eternity with the saints in heaven, where it is so much their work to praise God. The saints are sensible what cause they have to praise God and oftentimes are ready to say they long to praise Him more, and that they never can praise Him enough. This may be a consolation to you, that you shall have a whole eternity in which to praise Him. They earnestly desire to praise God better.

This, therefore, may be your consolation, that in heaven your heart shall be enlarged, you shall be enabled to praise Him in an immensely more perfect and exalted manner than you can do in this world. You shall not be troubled with such a dead, dull heart, with so much coldness, so many clogs and burdens from corruption and from an earthly mind; with a wandering, unsteady heart; with so much darkness and so much hypocrisy. You shall be one of that vast assembly that praise God so fervently, that their voice is "as the voice of many waters, and as the voice of mighty thunderings."

You long to have others praise God, to have everyone praise Him. There there will be enough to help you and join you in praising Him, and those that are capable of doing it ten thousand times better than saints on earth. Thousands and thousands of angels and glorified saints will be around you, all united to you in the dearest love, all disposed to praise God, not only for themselves, but for His mercy to you.

Thanksgiving Obtains the Spirit

Robert Murray McCheyne (1813–1843) is one of the brightest lights of the Church of Scotland. Born in Dundee, he was educated in Edinburgh and licensed to preach in 1835. For a brief time, he assisted his friend, Andrew A. Bonar, at Larbert and Dunipace. In 1836 he was ordained and installed as pastor of St. Peter's Church, Dundee, where he served until his untimely death two months short of his thirtieth birthday. He was known for his personal sanctity and his penetrating ministry of the Word, and great crowds came to hear him preach. *The Memoirs and Remains of Robert Murray McCheyne,* by Andrew Bonar, is a Christian classic that every minister of the gospel should read.

This sermon is taken from *The Additional Remains of the Rev. Robert Murray McCheyne,* published in 1846 in Edinburgh by William Oliphant and Co. McCheyne preached it in St. Peter's Church, Dundee, on November 24, 1839, just after he returned from a missionary visit to Palestine.

Robert Murray McCheyne

6

THANKSGIVING OBTAINS THE SPIRIT

> It came even to pass, as the trumpeters and singers were as one, to make one sound to be heard in praising and thanking the Lord; and when they lifted up their voice with the trumpets and cymbals and instruments of music, and praised the Lord, saying, For he is good; for his mercy endureth forever: that then the house was filled with a cloud, even the house of the Lord; so that the priests could not stand to minister by reason of the cloud; for the glory of the Lord had filled the house of God (2 Chronicles 5:13–14).

THE DAY HERE spoken of appears to have been a day of days. It seems to have been the day of Pentecost in Old Testament times—a type of all the glorious days of an outpoured Spirit that ever have been in the world—a foretaste of that glorious day when God will fulfill that amazing, soul-satisfying promise: "I will pour out my Spirit upon all flesh."

My dearly beloved flock, it is my heart's desire and prayer that this very day might be such a day among us—that God would indeed open the windows of heaven, as He has done in times past, and pour down a blessing, till there be no room to receive it.

Let us observe, then, how thanksgiving brings down the Spirit of God.

1. How the People Were Engaged

"In praising and thanking the Lord." Yea, you have their very words: "For he is good; for his mercy endureth forever." It was thus the people were engaged when the cloud came down and filled the house. They had been engaged in many other most affecting duties. The Levites had been carrying the ark from Mount Zion and placing it under the wings of the cherubim; Solomon and all his people had been offering sacrifices, sheep and oxen, which could not be told for multitude—still no answer came from heaven. But when the trumpeters and singers were as one in praising and thanking the Lord, when they lifted up their voices, saying: "For he is good; for his mercy endureth forever"—then the windows of heaven were opened—then the cloud came down and filled the whole temple.

My dear flock, I am deeply persuaded that there will be no full, soul-filling, heart-ravishing, heart-satisfying, outpouring of the Spirit of God till there be more praise and thanking the Lord. Let me stir up your hearts to praise.

He is good. Believers should praise God for what He is in Himself. Those that have never seen the Lord cannot praise Him. Those that have not come to Christ have never seen the King in His beauty. An unconverted man sees no loveliness in God. He sees a beauty in the blue sky—in the glorious sun—in the green earth—in the spangling stars—in the lily of the field; but he sees no beauty in God. He has not seen Him, neither known Him; therefore there is no melody of praise in that heart. When a sinner is brought to Christ, he is brought to the Father. Jesus gave Himself for us, "that he might bring us to God." O! what a sight breaks in upon the soul—the infinite, eternal, unchangeable God! I know that some of you have been brought to see this sight. Oh! praise Him, then, for what He is. Praise Him for His *pure, lovely holiness* that cannot bear any sin in His sight. Cry, like the angels, "Holy, holy, holy, Lord God Almighty." Praise Him for His *infinite wisdom* that He knows the end from the beginning. In Him are hid all the treasures of wisdom and knowledge. Praise Him for His *power*—that all matter, all mind, is in His hand. The heart of the king, the heart of saint and sinner, are all in His hand. Hallelujah! for the Lord God Omnipotent reigns. Praise Him for His *love*; for God is love. Some of you have been at sea. When far out of sight of land, you have stood high on the vessel's prow and looked round and round—one vast circle of ocean without any bound. Oh! so it is to stand in Christ justified, and to behold the love of God—a vast ocean all around you without a bottom and without a shore. Oh! praise Him for what He is. Heaven will be all praise. If you cannot praise God, you never will be there.

For His mercy—for what He has done for us. The Lord has done much for me since I parted from you. We were once in perils of waters; but the Lord saved the ship. Again and again we were in danger of plague—we nightly heard the cry of the mourner; yet no plague came near our dwelling. Again and again we were in perils of robbers—the gun of the murderous has been leveled at us; but the Lord stayed his hand. I have been at the gates of death since we parted. No one that saw me would have believed that I could be here this day; yet He has healed our diseases and brought me back to open once more to you the unsearchable riches of Christ. I, then, have reason to praise Him; for His mercy endures forever. The Lord has done much for you since we parted. My eyes filled with tears when I left you; for I thought He had done it in anger. I thought it was anger to me, and I thought it was anger to you; but now I see it was all love—it was all mercy to unworthy you and to unworthy me. The Lord gave you my dear brother to care for your souls and far better than that—for to give you a man only would have been a poor gift—but He has given you His Holy Spirit. "Bless the Lord, O my soul!" Praise Him, O my people! for He is good; for His mercy endures forever.

Are there not some of you brands plucked out of the burning? You were in the burning; the pains of hell were actually getting hold on you. You had a hell in your own hearts—you had a hell yawning to receive you; but the Lord snatched you from the burning. Will you not praise Him? Are there not some of you whom I left blind and deaf and dumb and dead? You saw no beauty in Him who is fairer than the children of men; you saw no glory in Immanuel—God manifest in flesh. But the Lord has said: "Go, wash in the pool of Siloam"; and whereas you were blind, now you see. Oh! praise Him that has done it. In heaven, they praise God most of all for this: "Worthy is the Lamb that was slain." Oh! have you no praise for

Jesus for all His love for the Father—for the Spirit? Some
of you cannot sing: "No man could learn that song but
those that were redeemed from the earth." Some of you
are worse than when I left you. You have resisted me—
you have resisted my brother; and, oh! worse than all, you
have resisted the Holy Spirit. You are prayerless yet—
Christless yet. Ah! unhappy souls! unredeemed, unre-
newed, remember it will be too late to learn to praise
when you die. You must begin now. I will tell you what a
dear friend of my own once said before dying. She desired
all the servants to be brought in; and she said very sol-
emnly: "There's nothing but Christ between me and weeping and wailing and gnashing of teeth. Oh! if you have
not Christ, then there is nothing between you and weeping and wailing and gnashing of teeth." You that will not
praise Christ now, shall wail because of Him soon.

2. The Manner of Their Praise

They were "as one." Their hearts were all as one heart
in this exercise. There were a thousand tongues, but only
one heart. Not only were their harps and cymbals and
dulcimers all in tune, giving out a harmonious melody,
but their hearts were all in tune. God had given them one
heart, and then the blessing came down. The same was
the case on the day of Pentecost; they were all with *one
accord* in one place; they were looking to the same Lamb
of God. The same thing will be the case in that day proph-
esied of in Psalm 133:1–3: "Behold, how good and how
pleasant it is for brethren to dwell together in unity! . . .
there God commands the blessing, even life forevermore."
This is the very thing which Jesus prayed for in that
prayer which none but God could have asked, and none
but God could answer: "Neither pray I for these alone, but
for them also which shall believe on me through their
word; that they all may be one; as thou, Father, art in me,
and I in thee, that they also may be one in us; that the
world may believe that thou hast sent me." And then
follows the blessing: "And the glory which thou gavest me
I have given them; that they may be one, even as we are
one: I in them, and thou in me, that they may be made

perfect in one; and that the world may know that thou has sent me, and hast loved them, as thou hast loved me."

Dear children of God, unite your praises. Let your hearts no more be divided. You are divided from the world by a great gulf. Soon it will be an infinite gulf; but you are united to one another by the same Spirit—you have been chosen by the same free, sovereign love—you have been washed in the same precious blood—you have been filled by the same blessed Spirit. Little children, love one another. He that loves is born of God. Be one in your praises. Join in one cry: "Worthy is the Lamb that was slain: thou art worthy to open the book—thou art worthy to reign in our hearts." And, oh! be fervent in praise. Lift up your voices in it—lift up your hearts in it. In heaven they wax louder and louder. John heard the sound of a great multitude, and then it was like many waters, and then it was like mighty thunderings, crying: "Hallelujah! hallelujah!" I remember Edwards' remark, that it was in the singing of praises that his people felt themselves most enlarged, and that then God was worshiped somewhat in the beauty of holiness. Let it be so among yourselves. Learn, dearly beloved, to praise God heartily—to sing with all your heart and soul in the family and in the congregation. But, oh! remember that even your praises must be sprinkled with blood and can be acceptable to God only by Jesus Christ.

3. The Effects of Their Praise

The cloud filled the house. This cloud is the very same which led them through the Red Sea and went before them forty years in the wilderness. It was a pillar of cloud by day, to shade them from the heat; it was a pillar of fire by night, to guide Israel on their way to the promised rest; and now it came and filled the holiest of all and the holy place. Such was the wonderful effect which followed their united fervent praises. God Himself came down and filled every chamber of the house with His presence. "This is my rest forever: here will I dwell; for I have desired it." Now, my dear friends, we are not now to expect that God will answer our prayers or follow our praises with a pillar of cloud or a pillar of fire. These were but the shadows; now we receive the reality—the substance. If you will but unite in unanimous and heartfelt praises, then am I persuaded that God will give His Holy Spirit to fill this house—to fill every heart in the spiritual temple. How glorious this will be:

For the children of God—are there not some of you who have come to Christ, and nothing more? Guilty, weary, heavy laden, you have found rest—redemption through His blood—even the forgiveness of sins. Oh! do not stop there. Do not rest in mere forgiveness—cry for the indwelling of the Holy Spirit, the Comforter. Forgiveness is but a means to an end. You are justified in order that you may be sanctified. Remember, without holiness you will never see the Lord; and without this indwelling Spirit, you never will be holy.

Are there not some of you groaning under a body of sin and death and crying with the apostle, "Oh! wretched man, who shall deliver me from the body of this death?" Do you not feel the plague of your own heart? Do you not feel the power of your old nature? How many in this state lean upon themselves—trust in their resolutions—attempt, as it were by force, to put down their sins! But here is the remedy. Oh! cry for the flood-tide of God's Spirit, that He may fill every chamber of your heart—that He may renew you in the spirit of your mind.

Are there not many who are cold, worldly Christians—those who were long ago converted but have fallen sadly back under the power of the world—either its gaiety or its business, its mirth or its money—and they have got into worldly habits, deep ruts of sin? Ah! see what you need. He that created humanity in His own image at first must create you over again. You need an almighty indwelling Comforter. Oh! it is He only who can melt your icy heart and make it flow out in love to God—who can fill you with all the fullness of God.

Are there not some who read the Bible but get little from it? You feel that it does not sink into your heart—it does not remain with you through the week. It is like the seed cast in the wayside, easily plucked away. Oh! it is just such an outpoured Spirit you require to hide the Word in your heart. When you write with a dry pen without any ink in it, no impression is made upon the paper. Now, ministers are the pens, and the Spirit of God is the ink. Pray that the pen may be filled with that living ink—that the Word may remain in your heart, known and read of all—that you may be sanctified through the truth.

For the unconverted—so it was in the day of Pentecost—the Spirit came first upon the small company of disciples and then on the three thousand. You have seen the hills attracting the clouds and so drawing down the shower into the valleys—so do God's children, having their heads within the veil, obtain the Spirit of God in fullness and dispense it to all around. You have seen some tall tree or spire catching the lightning and conveying it down into the ground—so does the fire of God's Spirit come first upon the trees of righteousness and from them descends to the dead souls around them.

A word to dead souls—keep near to God's children at such a time as this. Do not separate from them—do not mock at them; you may yet receive the grace of God through them. Dear believers, for the sake of the dead souls around you—for the sake of this great town, full of wickedness—for the sake of our land, filled with formality and hypocrisy—oh! unite in prayer and unite in praise and prove the Lord, if He will not pour out a blessing. Not for your own sakes only, but for the sake of those perishing around you, let us wrestle and pray for a fuller time of the Spirit's working than has ever been seen in Scotland yet.

The priests could not stand to minister. Before the cloud came down, no doubt the priests were all busily engaged burning incense and offering sacrifices; but when the cloud came down, they could only wonder and adore. So it ever will be when the Lord gives much of His Spirit; He will make it evident that it is not the work of human beings. If He were to give only a little, then ministers would begin to think they had some hand in it; but when He fills the house, then He makes it plain that man has nothing to do with it. David Brainerd said that when God awakened his whole congregation of Indians, he stood by amazed and felt that he was as nothing—that God alone was working. Oh! it is this, dear friends, that we desire and pray for—that the Lord the Spirit would Himself descend and with His almighty power tear away the veil from your hearts, convince you of sin, of righteousness, and of judgment—that Jesus Himself would take His scepter and break your hearts and take all the glory—that we may cry out: "Not unto us, Lord, not unto us, but unto thy name give glory."

NOTES

Sacrifice and Song

George H. Morrison (1866–1928) assisted the great
Alexander Whyte in Edinburgh, pastored two churches,
and then became pastor in 1902 of the distinguished
Wellington Church on University Avenue in Glasgow. His
preaching drew great crowds; in fact, people had to line
up an hour before the services to be sure to get seats in
the large auditorium. Morrison was a master of
imagination in preaching, yet his messages are solidly
biblical.

From his many published volumes of sermons, I have
chosen this message, found in *The Return of the Angels*,
published in 1909 by Hodder and Stoughton, London.

George H. Morrison

7

SACRIFICE AND SONG

And when the burnt-offering began, the song of the Lord began also (2 Chronicles 29:27).

HEZEKIAH WAS AN excellent monarch although he had a very vicious father. We have a proverb which says "like father like son," but that is far from being always true. Eli, a good and pious man, had sons who were a byword for profanity; and Ahaz, who was a rebel against God, had God-fearing Hezekiah for his child. In the first month of the first year of his reign Hezekiah opened the doors of the Temple. He recognized that social prosperity runs its roots down into religion. Then there followed these memorable scenes, of which our chapter gives a vivid summary, and in which the recreant and fickle multitude were brought into new fellowship with God. First there were the offerings for sin, for the people were defiled and needed cleansing. It was a scene of blood around the altars, dimly foreshadowing the blood of Jesus. Then, following these offerings for sin, burnt-offerings were laid upon the altar, and when the burnt-offering began, the song of the Lord began also.

Now, do you know what the burnt-offering meant? It meant the consecration of the life. It meant the giving up of self to Him in whose name the altar had been built. It was not typical of sin forgiven—the sin-offering was the rite for that. It was typical of the devotion of the life which must follow pardon, if pardon be reality. And the point to note is that in the very moment when the flame of the burnt-offering leaped heavenward, in that very moment there was a burst of music that echoed and re-echoed through the courts. It was not mournful music; it was glad. It was preeminently the music of the Lord. It stirred the hearts of the assembled crowd. It thrilled them to the finest fiber of their beings. And some who had been depressed took heart again, and some who had been fearful were encouraged, and some whose eyes had been bedewed with tears were quickened into the liberty of joy.

Now in that ancient and dramatic scene have we not a parable of living truths? I think that always when the burnt-offering begins, the song of the Lord begins also. Wherever there is devotion, there is gladness. Where there is consecration, there is music. Let a man be ignorant of self-surrender, and under the fairest sky he will be miserable. But let him devote himself with heart and soul to his duty, to his calling, to his God; and voices that were silent yesterday will break forth into singing as he moves.

We see that, for instance, in the case of work—in the case of the daily tasks that we are called to. There is always a lack of gladness in our work when we set about it in a grumbling way. It is one of the most common complaints today that people are not in earnest with their work. Their one ambition is to get it done and done as cheaply and easily as possible. That is a very bad thing for the work; but I think it is a worse thing for the worker, for to go to our work in a halfhearted way is a certain recipe to miss the music. It is not by doing less that joy will come, nor necessarily will it come by doing more. It is by throwing ourselves on our tasks with all our might, whether the task be little or be great. That is the spirit which makes labor glad and wakens the song that sleeps on the breast of drudgery and brings that light into the eyes of toil, which is brighter than the sunniest morn of May.

I think, too, that this is very true in regard to the great matter of our cross-bearing. It is not till the burnt-offering begins that we ever hear a single strain of music. Every human life has got its shadow, and every human life has got its cross. It is well to distinguish the shadow from the cross, lest by confusing them we go astray. For the shadow is something into which we enter and out of which we shall pass in God's good time. But the cross is something that we must take up, or stumble over into the mouth of hell. Now one of the deepest questions in life is, "In what way do you regard your crosses?" Do you hate them? Do you rebel against them? Would you give anything to fling them from you? Along that road there is no voice of song. Along that road there is the hardening heart. Along that road there is a growing bitterness, the foretaste of the bitterness of death. But take up your cross, as Jesus bids you do—take it up as a mother takes her child. Lay it against your heart and cherish it—say "This, too, like the summer roses, is from God." And so shall your poor life become a harmony—and what is harmony but perfect music—and when the burnt-offering begins, the song of the Lord will begin also.

But once again, is not our text illuminative in regard to our social relationships? To be selfish there is not to miss the worry. To be selfish is to miss the song. Look at the mother with her little child. She was a thoughtless girl just a few years ago. Now she would lay her life down for her infant, and, what is better than dying, she would live for it. She has begun to offer her burnt-offering, to surrender everything for love's sweet sake, and you have only to look into her eyes to see that with the offering has come the song.

> Love took up the harp of life and
> smote on all the chords with might,
> Smote the chord of self that, trembling,
> passed in *music* out of sight.

An inferior poet would have said in *tears*; but Tennyson was too wise for such an error. He knew that when self is overcome by love, it is to the sound of music that it dies. Have we not all known people—and not always young people—who had well-nigh everything this world could give them? Yet you would never dream of envying them or of thinking that their lives were glad or rich. And there are others, whose lot is far from easy and whose heaven to our eyes is very gray, and yet they seem like singing all the time. I shall tell you why so many lives are songless. It is because they have never got the length of the burnt-offering. They never think of others—never plan for others—never deny themselves in little things for others. And of all self-denials those are hardest which in the eyes of others might seem easiest. It is often the surrendering of little things that is more difficult than the surrender of the great. I am not asking you to die for people, but I am asking you to live for people. For your mother, for your husband, for your wife, for your brother, for your sister, for your child. God knows how selfish you have been. God knows you ought to be ashamed of it. Will you begin to offer the burnt-offering? Then the song of the Lord will begin also.

Then, in closing, does not our text hold true of what is especially the *Christian* life? To be halfhearted toward Jesus Christ is the most tragic of all conditions. Other masters might be content with that. Christ will have none of it—He scorns it. It must be first or nowhere, all or nothing—king or nobody, with Jesus Christ. And the strange thing is when we take Him at His word and give ourselves up to Him in glad devotion, then when the burnt-offering begins, the song of the Lord begins also. You know, you halfhearted followers of Christ—you know there is no joy in your religion. You are trying to carry your religion, and your religion was meant to carry you. Give Jesus Christ His lawful place tonight. Say, "Lord, I lay myself upon the altar." And you will find that the way of the burnt-offering is vocal with the gladness of the song.

NOTES

Praise Comely to the Upright

Charles Haddon Spurgeon (1834–1892) is undoubtedly the most famous minister of the last century. Converted in 1850, he united with the Baptists and soon began to preach in various places. He became pastor of the Baptist church in Waterbeach in 1851, and three years later he was called to the decaying Park Street Church, London. Within a short time the work began to prosper, a new church was built and dedicated in 1861, and Spurgeon became London's most popular preacher. In 1855 he began to publish his sermons weekly; and today they make up the fifty-seven volumes of *The Metropolitan Tabernacle Pulpit*. He founded a pastor's college and several orphanages.

This sermon is taken from *The Metropolitan Tabernacle Pulpit*, Volume 61 and was preached on June 18, 1868.

Charles Haddon Spurgeon

8

PRAISE COMELY TO THE UPRIGHT

Praise is comely for the upright (Psalm 33:1).

THE PSALMIST WAS full of praise and therefore felt that he could not fully express the glory of God but desired to enlist others in the sacred service. You hear him often calling upon sea and land, upon earth and heaven, upon mountain and valley, upon plants and creeping things, upon living creatures, upon the heavens and the heavens that are above the heavens, to assist him in magnifying the name of the Infinite Jehovah, whose praise still exceeds all the honor that can be given to Him by all His creatures. Praise has a blessed contagion in it. It is like fire; if it burns its way in one place, it will be spreading itself if it can. A man cannot praise God alone. There will always be within him a high ambition to teach others, to take up the strain. He will always be longing and desiring to lead others in the same sweet employ. Now let us seem to hear across these ages the voices of those who are with their God as they cry to us, "Rejoice in the lord, ye righteous, for praise is comely to the upright."

I have taken for a text that one sentence; and I will speak of it under four short words which may serve as headings—four words of question. The first is:

1. What?

What is it which is so comely, so comely to the upright? It is praise, the praise of God, and this praise of God, though it is always the same thing, the same spiritual thing produced by the Spirit of God, yet takes different forms, and in each form it is still comely to the upright. It is so in *that delightful form of music in which we express with accord, hearts and voices keeping tune together, in the great congregation our sense of united adoration.* I do think there is nothing more comely than the sweet songs of the sanctuary, and what our friends of the Society of Friends do without singing I scarcely know. I think they will have to recant that one thing at least when they enter heaven, for surely they cannot be silent there, where all shall join in songs like unto great thunder and like the mighty rolling of the sea in praise of the infinite majesty of Him who was slain, but who ever lives. I think we could not anyhow give up our song. We should feel as if the Sabbath were shorn of its bloom, as if you had plucked the flowers out of the garden of the soul. Our soul must sing, yea, she will sing praises unto the Lord. So natural does it seem to the renewed heart to join in praise with others that even when lying in the dungeon, after having been beaten sore with stripes and with their feet fast in the stocks, Paul and Silas did not only pray, but they sang praises unto God, and praise was comely there. It has been comely in many a prison where no one has heard the sound but God. It has been comely among the glens of Scotland, when the Covenanters lifted up the psalm. It has been comely in nooks and corners of England when Puritans in fear of their lives nevertheless magnified the name of the Lord. It has been comely at the stakes at Smithfield; comely from Anne Askew's lips when she was on the rack, stretched to the utmost. It has been comely anywhere when the voice has poured out itself with musical rhythm in the praise of the Most High.

But there is a second form of vocal praise which is equally comely to the upright—*the spoken praise* of God. I allude to those praises which consist of commendation of the name and person and service and goodness of the Lord by private Christians to their fellowmen. Think not that all praise is gathered up in singing. It is the praise of God when the mother tells her child of the goodness of Him who made the stars and who spread the world with flowers. It is praise when the young convert tells of the joy of his heart to his companion and bids him fly to the fountain where he has washed and been made clean. It is praise, praise of a high order, too, when the advanced believer in his old age tells of the faithfulness of God, and how not one good thing has failed of all that the Lord God has promised; and while praise seems to sit in such a comely manner upon the young convert that it seems to be the most natural thing in all the world for him to praise, it is equally comely in the aged Christian, for he seems to feel that if such a man as he, preserved so long, did not praise God, the very stones in the street would cry out against him.

That praise which consists in living, loving, personal testimony to the goodness and faithfulness of the Lord is always comely to the upright. I wish that some Christians would recollect that murmuring is not comely; that envying others, that finding fault, that ambition, that desiring greater things—that all these are not comely, but the speaking well of His name, the testimony to His faithfulness in providence and to His goodness in grace—this is comely to the upright.

But the truest praise, perhaps, is *that which is not expressed in language, because it could not be—meditative praise.* I fear there is but little of this in London. I am not sure that there is any more of it in the country, though there ought to be a great deal more of it in both. I mean such praise as this—when, like David, we sit before the Lord and think of His exceeding bounty, and then say, "What am I, and what is my Father's house that thou hast brought me hitherto?" I mean the praise that makes the tear unbidden come to the eye, not the tear of sorrow, but the tear of overwhelming gratitude for the goodness of God, so that the soul, without making use of words, seems to say:

> When all thy mercies, O my God,
> My rising soul surveys,
> Transported, with the view, I'm lost
> In wonder, love, and praise;

when thoughts become too heavy for words to carry them; when they break the backs of words, as it were; when "expressive silence," as the poet calls it, has to come to the rescue, and one is compelled rather to fall prostrate before the infinite majesty and goodness than to venture on a sonnet that would fall flat in the presence of such emotions.

> Words are but air, and tongues but clay,
> And thy compassions are divine.

Where, then, shall it be found possible for words and for tongues worthily to express thy praise? I am sure it would be a very refreshing thing to us all, acceptable to God and very blessed to ourselves, if we had more of this quiet praise, if we could get to some of those cool retreats, those silent shades, that do with prayer and praise agree and seem by God's kind bounty made for those who would worship Him. Such praise is comely to the upright. I like to think of George Herbert walking through the parsonage garden and up and down by the banks of the brook, singing within himself of his God, and of those other holy men and women who led meditative lives. It seems to fit them as a beautiful vest that is comely upon their shoulders when they are engaged in the meditative praise of God.

But one more remark. Sometimes praise does not even fall into the form of meditation, much less of conversation or of song; it becomes—what shall I call it?—*habitual praise—the spirit of praise.* I will indicate one or two brothers and sisters in this congregation who, if it were the depth of winter, would create a smile in my vestry if they would but enter it; who, whenever I meet them, their eyes sparkle like stars; their lips drop pearls; they never seem to be unhappy, never doubting, never distrustful. They are sure to speak every Sabbath morning, "We shall have a good day today; there has been much prayer about it, and God always answers prayer; you will be graciously helped through it; be of good courage"; and on Sunday night it is, "This has been a good Sunday." In fact, they say they never have anything but good Sabbaths; they always seem to be fed, and they are always rejoicing, and if you talk to them, they are not the youngest people in the congregation, perhaps; they may not be the richest, they may not be in the best circumstances, but they are always the most cheerful, always the most happy, and they can say:

> We would not change our blest estate
> For all the world calls good and great.

Now, believe me, I think this is most comely to the upright when men or women shall get into the spirit of praise so that they shall be always blessing God. Why, it is such a beautiful dress to wear that they shine in the family, they shine in business, they shine in the church, they shine in the eyes of angels, who think that they must be angels, too, they have got into such an angelic frame of mind. Such a man was Bernard Gilpin, who always said, "It was all for the best." If it was fair, it was all for the best; or if there had been any rain, it was all for the best. Were it hot or were it cold, it was all for the best. Bernard was arrested by the queen's order to be brought to London to be burned, but he said it was all for the best. The soldiers, knowing of this expression of his, jeered him all along the journey with blasphemies, and when his horse fell and he broke his leg, they laughed, but he said it was all for the best. He was laid upon the road for a surgeon to set his bones, but he said it was all for the best, and so it proved to be, for this delayed them, and when they got just within sight of London they could hear the bells ringing, and, on inquiry, they learned that Queen Mary was dead and Queen Elizabeth had succeeded; so that Mr. Bernard Gilpin had arrived in London just three days too late to be burned, and he was quite correct in saying that it was all for the best. But I have no doubt that if he had gone to the stake he would have said it was all for the best, and certainly his emancipated spirit, as it left its charred ashes behind, would have sung, "Yes, it is all for the best." Now that state of heart, not the act of praise but the spirit of praise in which the soul seems to swim in praise, as the fish swims in the river, and to bathe and perfume itself with thanksgiving as Esther perfumed herself in Ahasuerus' palace—such a state of heart as this is extremely comely to the upright. That is the answer to the question—What? The next question is:

2. Why?

Why is praise so befitting and becoming to the upright? We answer that it is so, and you will soon see it, *from the nature of things*. Wings are most becoming to an angel. You would not think of drawing one of those spirits that are like flames of fire without giving it wings. What for? Why, to mount with, to make him ethereal, to quicken his motions. Well, and the Christian without praise would be without his wings. What is he to mount with? He does not wish to grovel here below, fond of these earthly toys, but how is he to mount? Prayer gives him one wing, but praise must give him the other, and when he gets prayer and praise, oh! how he seems to leave sublunary things behind, and away he flies, borne by the strong help of the eternal Spirit up to:

> Where eternal ages roll,
> Where solid pleasures never die,
> And fruits immortal feast the soul.

Take away the Christian's power of praising God, and you make him a poor earthworm, bound here with doubts and fears and cares; but let him but kindle in his soul the flame that burns in heaven of seraphic love to God, and away he mounts.

Praise is comely to the upright, in the next place, *from the office of the believer*. When Aaron put on his breastplate, his girdle, his ephod, and his bells, everyone said that the garment was comely to Aaron. It would not have been comely to us because we should have no right to wear it, but the office of Aaron made it comely to him. You would not think it comely if I were to come here to preach to you tonight with a red coat on. You would have said, "No, that red coat is exceedingly comely to the soldier; it suits him; but it does not suit the minister." Now the Christian is a priest, and praise is a part of the garment of a priest that he must wear. Praise is the employment of a priest. Inasmuch as we are kings and priests unto God, it becomes us that we should swing that golden censer that is full of thanksgiving, and that we should stand before the golden altar and continually offer sacrifice and praise acceptable to God by Jesus Christ. It suits our nature and suits our office, and therefore it is comely to the upright.

Praise is comely to the upright, *as flowers and fruits are comely to a plant*. There never was a plant but what the fruit it bore suited it, and the greatest comeliness to the apple tree in the garden is to see it loaded with its wondrous blossoms, the most beautiful things in all the world, and then afterward to see the boughs hanging down with luscious fruit. The comeliness of a plant lies in its coming to perfection and bearing its fruit. So with Christians. The barren Christian has no comeliness, but the comeliness of the Christian, his spiritual comeliness, lies in his bringing forth fruit unto God, and what is this but praise? "Whoso offereth praise glorifieth me," says the Lord. Man is made on purpose to glorify God. It is his chief end. Then his chief end is comely to him. If he answers his end, he is comely to Him who made him, and inasmuch as our chief end is to glorify God, praise becomes comely to the upright.

Once again praise is comely to the upright *as a crown is comely to a king*. It is his highest honor, his chief dignity. It is one of our highest honors to praise God—praise Him that we are His elected, His begotten; that we are His redeemed, His sanctified, His preserved people. When we get to this we occupy as high a stand as we well can do short of heaven, and in heaven I know not if we shall ever seem more comely than when we are, with all the hosts of angels, praising and magnifying the name of the Lord. When we praise God we do, as it were, put on our crowns, as when they before the throne praise God they also come with their crowns but make it part of their praise to put them off again with, "Not unto us, not unto us, O Lord, but unto thy name be glory!"

Now, Christian, just treasure up this thought, that praise is comely to the upright. There are a great many people in the world who think a great deal of their personal appearance. How they will look in that glass! How they will turn that hair again! How they arrange that dress! There must not be a pin awry. What does it matter! After you have dressed yourselves as best you may, flies, bees, and insects of all kinds excel you still. When you have glorified yourselves to the pitch of Solomon, yet you cannot match the lilies; they still excel you. But that idea of comeliness ought to be turned into a better channel. If I want to make myself comely, why should I not desire to be comely in the esteem of those whose opinion is worth the having, and comely in the eyes of God? How can this be, then? Well, if I have, first of all, been covered with the blood and righteousness of Jesus Christ, which are the true beauty of the Christian, then the next thing to make me comely is to praise God, to keep His praises continually on my lips. If I begin complaining and mourning when I am hardly dealt by, I am, as it were, but scratching my own face; it is not comely to me; I am putting on rags; I am soiling my garments; I am pulling off my gold rings; I am stripping myself of my ornaments. But if I praise God then I am acting according to my better nature, according to my office; I am acting in the most honorable capacity possible, and I am answering the end for which God made me. Do, therefore, you who want to be thought comely, be continually praising God.

And now, in the third place, another little word to help your memories, and that shall be:

3. When?

"Praise is comely to the upright"; but when? Now-a-days that which is comely one day is not comely the next, for the fashions change so continually. But let me tell you that the spiritual fashions never alter, and that which God declares to be comely today will be comely next year and comely forever. Praise is never out of fashion, never out of season, never out of date. You may praise God and utter even the same sentiments as came from the lips of Enoch, and there shall be nothing stale therein; still, it shall be comely. When is it comely for Christians to praise God? My answer is *always*. I must comprehend all seasons and all places. It is never uncomely to praise God. When the congregation have met, and the service has commenced, it is the time to lift up the voice unanimously; oh! it is comely then to the believer to praise the Most High God. If there be but two or three who are met together in some lowly schoolroom or a shed or a hall or under the forest trees, or half a dozen on the deck of a vessel or down in the cabin or the forecastle—it matters not where, let us pitch our tent and sing one of the songs of Zion. Praise is comely to the upright from half a dozen in some backwoods settlement or out in the bush at a settler's log-hut. Sweet everywhere, it is unacceptable nowhere. Praise is in all such places comely when the saints come together. And, brethren, praise is comely from the Christian *at any season.* If he wakes in the morning, he sings:

> Awake! lift up thyself, my heart,
> And with the angels bear thy part,
> Who all night long unwearied sing
> High praises to the Eternal King.

His morning praise, glistening with dew, is comely. And if in the night-watches he tosses restlessly on the bed, why, praise at night again is sweet, and so will it be from the believer if he can sing the praises of the Lord then. When you are cracking your whip, you that drive a cart in the streets, why, you can sing one of the songs of Zion there. There is many a light and frothy song sung there; why should not ours be sung too? It will be comely to the upright. When you are in the field digging, plowing, haymaking, harvesting; when you good girls are at work at the needle or the sewing machine or book-folding or whatever it is; you mothers, rocking your cradles or whatever it may be—praise will not seem out of place if you be upright in heart. Praise will be comely to you on all occasions then.

But there are *certain occasions when praise has a peculiar beauty.* For instance, praise is comely to the upright when you are in poverty. It is easy to praise God when you have all you want. Who would not? A dog will follow you when you feed him. But to praise God when He takes away those gifts that you prize the most—oh! this is comely praise indeed. To say with Job, "Though he slay me, yet will I trust in him; shall we receive good from the hand of the Lord, and shall we not receive evil?"—that is praise. Let me just say that when we lie upon the bed and pain shoots through us, some of us who are a great deal more impatient than others are, do not find it very easy to praise God then, and yet oh! it is blessed when we can screw the harp-strings at last and get them right and bless the Lord that lives, who will yet bring us up from languishing and restore us from the gates of the grave. Praise in the midst of bodily pain—headache, heartache, or any form of disease, is very comely to the upright. And to praise God when some beloved one on whom your heart is set is sick—that is hard, but it is very comely. To see him on whom all your earthly dependence is fixed sickening and pining and yet to say, "The Lord's will be done, and blessed be His name," oh! 'tis so comely that I do not know that the angels in heaven have any of them such a piece of praise, so rich and rare as that of the song of resignation when beloved ones are going. And when the earth rattles on the coffin-lid of a dear child or a friend or a wife beloved, then to be able to say, "The Lord gave, and the Lord hath taken away, and blessed be the name of the Lord"—such praise as that is very comely to the upright. And when these things meet—when deaths and sickness and poverty come like many seas meeting at one place, let me tell you that the harder it is to sing, the more comely it is to do it. There is no music, perhaps, that we relish so much as the song of the nightingale, and that is because it sings in the night, and there is no praise more acceptable to God than the songs of His people in the night when they can praise Him under distress. I have read a saying by an old writer that God's birds sing best in cages, and so they do when the cages have in them some affliction and trial. Then do they pour out their notes sweetly, magnifying the name of the Lord. If I am asked, then, when should the believer praise God, I say, especially in the time of trial.

I may say yet again, that we never praise God, I think, so acceptably as *when others are blaspheming and profaning His name*. For the believer then to venture his testimony in the teeth of all defiance, to thrust himself in the way of jeers and sneers for Christ's sake, to bless God when others curse Him—this is very comely to a cross-bearer, to a servant of Him who laid down His life for His Father's glory. And in times when you come to be slandered, and your name is evil spoken of, and your religion is said to be rant, and your actions misrepresented, and your motives misconstrued—it is a grand thing then to praise God, and say:

> If on my face, for thy dear name,
> Shame and reproach shall be;
> I'll hail reproach and welcome shame,
> If thou remember me.

At such times, again, praise is sweet.

But, beloved, there is an hour coming when praise will be comeliest of all—I mean *when this mortal frame shall dissolve*, and our spirits shall be entering upon an unseen world. It is not every believer that dies singing. It is not necessary to his safety that he should do so, but oh! it is so comely if he can do it. As music is said to sound very sweetly over the water, so certainly over the billows of death the song of the triumphant Christian comes with special sweetness. I shall ever recollect with great delight one verse of a hymn which I heard from a dying Christian, who had become blind just before his death, and which has always since been invested in my recollections with a melody I never heard in it before:

> And when ye see my eyestring break,
> How sweet my minutes roll;
> A mortal paleness on my cheek,
> But glory in my soul.

Ah! it is comely to the upright to be praising God when heart and flesh are failing.

But I must leave that, and I shall finish with another little word, and that is:

4. Whom?

Praise is comely—not to everybody—but to the upright. It is a very sad reflection that during this week some of the most glorious music that ever was composed to some of the noblest words that have ever been written has been sung—and I do not altogether disapprove of it—but sung, I fear, by some who have no part nor lot in what they are singing. I refer to Handel's glorious music—the noblest sounds, I think, next to the songs of angels, and one of the highest and holiest enjoyments of earth to listen to. But there are singers there who know nothing of God or of His praise. It is very sad to think of it, but then it is just the same here on Sunday—just the same. You sing, but you do not sing. The sound is there, but not the heart in the song. As for your professional singing on Sabbath, I do believe that that is earthly, sensual, devilish outright. We have heard say of our friends in America that in some of their churches the choir is so much esteemed and so highly esteems itself that if the congregation were to sing they would almost frown upon them to put them out of tune, and that there is very little sound of the congregation's singing heard compared with those half a dozen perhaps as wicked singers as the music-halls could find, stuck up there to glorify God by insulting Him. There has been a good deal of that done in England too. Some of our churches have gone and picked up people according to their sweet voices and have said, "Now you praise God at so much per week." But the thing won't do; every conscience is convinced that it is wrong, and the text condemns it utterly, for praise is comely to the upright; it is not comely to anybody else.

The upright. Do you notice that word? It is a grand word, that word *upright*. It is not the man who goes out of his way hither and thither; it is not the crooked man; it is the upright man. Nobody praises God like the man that stands upright. God will have a straight musical instrument; He will not have it crooked. If we are to praise Him, we must be upright. And mark, being upright consists in perfect independence of all except God. The upright man does not lean on anything else, but stands right straight up. Now when a man says, "I should like to be a Christian, but—"; you are not upright. "I would be honest, but—"; you are not upright. "I would make a profession of religion, but—"; you are not upright. He who has two objects, two ends, who holds with the world and holds with God, is not upright, and he cannot praise God. But when a man has been created anew in Christ Jesus, when he has been taught what the right path is and has grace given him to follow it, and who says, "Now, come fair or come foul, my trust is in the living God; I would not lie, though it were to gain a world; nor would I cheat, though it were to win heaven itself; I am independent of these things, seeing that God has promised that He will never leave me, nor forsake me"—when a man thus stands upright he makes very blessed music, and such as God's ears accept. But your crooked tradesmen and your merchants that can cheat and your sneaks and your fraudulent bankrupts and I know not what besides—God wants no music out of them. It is no credit to a man to be praised by a rogue, and it is no credit to God to be praised by a man who has no character. When a man has character and lives up to it as a Christian man, then it becomes honorable to God to be praised by him. If I heard a bad man speak well of God, I should say, "Ah! I do not like that; as a jewel of gold set in a swine's snout, so is a good word from such a man as that." I am sure, if I lived near any of you and esteemed your character very highly, and I heard all the blacklegs in London say what a good soul you were, I should begin to ask if you had not done something amiss, if you had not done something wrong. Said one of the philosophers when he was praised by a bad man, "What have I done wrong that I should deserve to be praised by such a man as this?" and when ungodly men praise God we might almost say, "What has God done that such an one as this should praise Him?" Praise is not comely to such; it does not seem right at all. It is either a mere form without life and consequently a dead thing that God cannot accept, or else it is hypocritical, and God will not accept that; or else it is a downright insult, and that is to be avoided above all things. Praise is comely to the upright.

Then, my dear friends, are you upright? Have you, first of all, been laid flat and brought to the horizontal? If so, then you will soon come to the perpendicular. A man must be brought to lie flat before the throne of grace, confessing his own nothingness, and he must look up to the cross of Christ and rest there, or else he has not learned yet what it is to stand upright, for this alone can produce stability of principle—faith in the living God, and the believing man stands where all others fall. Oh! to have this uprightness of heart. If you have it, then go and praise God. It is comely to you. Cease not from it, but say, in the words of our hymn:

> I'll praise him in life, I'll raise him in death;
> I'll praise him as long as he lendeth me breath;
> And say when the death-dew lies cold on my brow,
> 'If ever I loved thee, my Jesus, 'tis now.'

Amen.

NOTES

He Delights in Our Gratitude

William E. Sangster (1900–1960) was the "John Wesley of his generation" as he devoted his life to evangelism and the promotion of practical sanctification. He pastored in England and Wales, and his preaching ability attracted the attention of the Methodist leaders. He ministered during World War II at Westminster Central Hall, London, where he pastored the church, managed an air-raid shelter in the basement, and studied for his Ph.D. at the London University. He served as president of the Methodist Conference (1950) and director of the denomination's home missions and evangelism ministry. He published several books on preaching, sanctification, and evangelism, as well as volumes of sermons.

This message comes from *Westminster Sermons*, Volume 2, published in 1961 by The Epworth Press, London.

William E. Sangster

9

HE DELIGHTS IN OUR GRATITUDE

. . . and he took the seven loaves and the fishes; and he gave thanks (Matthew 15:36).

SO FAR AS thanksgiving is concerned, the mass of people can be divided into two classes: those who take things for granted and those who take things with gratitude.

It is my aim today to add to the number of those who take things with gratitude.

Notice, first, that it is the *right* thing to do. To take benefits from God or man without a thought or a word of thanks is mean, contemptible, and undermines faith in human nature. When a man has been treated by a fellowman with ingratitude, the milk of human kindness curdles in him. He says afterward, "He never so much as said 'Thank you.' Even a dog would have wagged his tail."

Not only is it the right thing to do; it is the *profitable* thing to do. Oh no, I am not thinking cynically, like Sir Robert Walpole, when he said that "gratitude is a lively sense of future favors." I don't mean "profitable" in the sense that if you thank somebody you are more likely to get help from him again. I mean "profitable" in the sense that a man who is quick to mark and swift to thank a kindness is in a constant state of happiness and goodwill. He has a barricade built against depression. He faces life buoyantly and confidently because he is aware of mercy streaming on him from Heaven and from his fellowmen as well.

So give thanks!

Jesus is our example in this as in all things. He was constantly giving thanks.

I admit that it isn't always easy to give thanks. "How can you thank God for a cancer?" you might ask. Looked at like that, it is difficult, I know—though, in fact, the only people with cancer to whom I spoke last week both thanked God fervently for His mercies toward them. I am going to say this. To a Christian, even *this* quality of thanksgiving is gloriously possible. To those mature in the Christian faith, mercies can still be found near the heart of tragedy.

Oh, I know that there is a grotesque way of looking at it; a form of thanks which is not really thanks at all.

I heard the other day of a little girl—an unusual little girl in some ways and a naughty little girl as well—who detested milk pudding and had been made to eat some at her dinner. When she asked if she might get down from the table she was told to return thanks.

"But I have nothing to be thankful for," she said sulkily.

"Very well," said her mother. "Remain there until you have."

There was silence for a few minutes. Then a little voice said: "Thank God I wasn't sick. *Now* may I get down?"

I need hardly say that that is not the freakish attitude of mind I am commending. Rather, it is this: If, as the Bible teaches, "the steps of a good man are ordered by the Lord," a mature Christian will thank God even in trouble, the heaviest and most desolating trouble, that, though God did not "lead" him into sickness, he is not deserted in it; that, though he cannot see it as yet, he has faith to believe that somewhere there is mercy at the heart of it, or good that can come out of it; that it is, indeed, only another of the "all things" that still "work together for good to them that love God." The prayer of thanksgiving at such a time may, indeed, be what the Scriptures call a "sacrifice of thanksgiving"; a thanksgiving that almost has blood upon it; an adoring venture of faith—believing in defiance of the God-denying look of things. But the mature will be able to offer even that, not easily but definitely. And the *sacrifice* of thanksgiving will be precious in God's sight.

Thank God that those times which strain faith so hard come only occasionally in life. For the most part we travel a sunlit road, and when we are unaware of the love of God it is often because we have not looked for it. To see the evidence of God's mercies you have only to look.

Let us look at them at this time of Harvest Festival; let us *stare* at them.

1. The Common Blessings—Commonly Overlooked

Let us thank God for the fecund earth. Not without toil and sweat and foresight and struggle have all these lovely things been drawn from the earth. God did not set us in the world to receive our food merely by wishing for it. It comes only by the sweat of someone's brow, but the sweat alone would be useless without the added blessing of God. Look, I say, at this wonderful display, and for all the kindly fruits of earth, be grateful.

Let us thank God for our five senses and for whatever measure of health we enjoy.

I met a depressed man one day who told me that he had nothing to be thankful for, so I said: "Well, I'm going visiting; come with me."

I was going to the institution for the poor aged sick. In the town where I then ministered it was an old-fashioned building, and its management left much to be desired; but the man came with me. It was not a public visiting day, but I got him in "on the nod," and he just came around the wards with me. From bed to bed we went, seeing a great many of these pitiable old people. Some were dim of sight, and some were quite blind. Some were hard of hearing, and some were quite deaf. Some were imbecile, and in some their reason was partly impaired. (They seemed almost the most pitiable cases of all because, in their lucid moments, they knew the truth about themselves, and that was hard to bear.)

I didn't say anything much to my companion. I had come to visit the poor souls themselves; he just followed me around.

When we were outside again I did not rub the moral in. I just shook hands with him, because I had other duties to do, and he parted from me saying: "I don't think I'll ever grumble again."

It was a simple device, just showing him people less fortunate than himself. He went away saying (I think) under his breath, "I can see. I can see the face of my dear ones. I can see the sunshine and the first flowers which come out from the hard, dark earth in the spring.

"I can hear. I can hear the song of birds, the blackbirds fluting in the orchard and the carefree laughter of little children.

"I have my reason unimpaired. I can think and plan and pray. I am not well off, but I have enough. I have a roof over my head and food that I have bought on my table. I have, at least, a little in reserve against a rainy day. . . ."

Almost (not quite), but almost every single soul in this church now can see and hear, and all of you (so far as I know) have your reason utterly unimpaired. Thank God for the common blessings commonly overlooked. Don't wait till you lose them to be grateful. Look about you now at this harvest display; think of the fruitful earth, the solid structure of the seasons, the framework of the universe shaped in love and given to men. These are common blessings if you like, and yet, if you lost them and could know your loss, you would give almost all the other things you have to recover them and marvel, in your deprivation, that when you had them you did not value them more.

Thank God for common blessings; for the harvest fully gathered in and the great harvest moon rising above; for the sudden smile of a friend met unexpectedly in a place where you did not expect to meet anyone you knew; thank God for home, for birthday anniversaries, for the bulge and mystery of stockings in the dark on Christmas morning; thank God for the loyalty of the family when they laugh at your old joke, told the fiftieth time, but tried out expectantly on the new guest; for all ordinary things, taken for granted when they ought to be taken with gratitude: Thank God! Thank God!

2. The Special Blessings—Soon, Alas, Forgotten

First, thanks to God for the common blessings—commonly overlooked; secondly, thanks to God for *the special blessings—soon, alas, forgotten.*

Special blessings? Yes, we have had them. We have *all* had them. You may not have recognized them as such at the time, but they were. I suppose it is more probable, however, that you *did* half-recognize them, but you forgot them so soon.

God never gives a blessing just for the hour. Every special blessing is not only for the hour itself but for the future. It is a pledge; it is as though God were to say, "I'll do this for you now, and then you will *always* know that you are the object of My love."

What a sad thing it is, therefore, that we forget so soon. That is why new dangers can startle you with fear and dismay. You have forgotten the past mercies. You would have been calm and confident in the presence of this new trouble if you had remembered vividly the old deliverance; if you had kept it fresh in mind and been able to say, "The God who delivered me then didn't deliver me then to desert me now." And yet you are fearful in the presence of this new possibility and might be as ignorant as some savage in the mid-most forest who did not know that he had a loving Father in heaven.

Remember old John Newton?

> His love in time past forbids me to think
> He'll leave me at last in trouble to sink.

St. Teresa was in a mood of deep depression one day. Saint though she was, I think she had forgotten for an hour the many deliverances that God had vouchsafed to her. So God came and said, "When did I ever fail thee? I am today what I have always been."

Make a practice of noting your special blessings. Be as thorough about it as a missionary I read about who was a most diligent man in prayer and a master of "method" too. He used to note carefully in little books the special blessings he received and the answers he had to his prayers. The little books are still preserved, I believe. On the last day of the year he would assess the answers. There were usually between 87 and 90 percent of plain, impressive answers to the prayers which he had offered, and even concerning the rest he would not have admitted that they had not been answered. He would have said about those: "In regard to these things, for some purpose known to my Father, the answer had to be 'Wait' or 'No.'"

Make a practice of thanking God for His goodness to you and thanking those also by whose hand the blessing came. It does people good to be thanked. It is amazing what you will do for others, as well as for your own soul, if you will follow this counsel of saying a sincere "Thank you."

Let me put that last point in a picture for you.

When the business depression in America was at its worst, a group of men sat in a room talking over the sad state of affairs, and one of them was a friend of mine, a Methodist minister, the Rev. Professor William L. Stidger of the School of Theology in Boston, Massachusetts. The conversation concerned the recession in trade and got more miserable every moment it went on. But as Thanksgiving Day was near—a great day in America— a minister present said, "I have got to preach on Thanksgiving Day. I want to say something affirmative. What can I say that is affirmative in a period of world depression like this?"

Stidger began to think of the blessings he had had in life and the things for which he was truly thankful. He remembered the woman who had taught him in the infants' school and of whom he had not heard for many years. Although it was the *infants'* school, he still remembered that she had gone out of her way to put a love of verse in him, and Stidger has loved verse all his life. So he wrote a letter of thanks to the old lady. This is the reply he had. It was written in the feeble scrawl of the old, and it began "My dear Willie." He was thrilled about that. Stidger was over fifty at the time and bald and a professor, and he didn't think there was anybody left in the world who would call him "Willie." It made him feel years younger right off. Here is the letter. I'll give it to you word for word:

> My dear Willie,
>   I cannot tell you how much your note meant to me. I
> am in my eighties, living alone in a small room, cooking

my own meals, lonely and, like the last leaf of autumn, lingering behind.

You will be interested to know that I taught in school for fifty years and yours is the first note of appreciation I ever received. It came on a blue-cold morning and it cheered me as nothing has in many years.

Stidger is not sentimental, but he wept over that note. Stidger thought of other people who had been kind to him. He remembered one of his old bishops who had been most helpful at the beginning of his ministry. The bishop was in retirement and had recently lost his wife. Stidger wrote a belated letter of thanks to the bishop. This was the reply:

My dear Will,

Your letter was so beautiful, so real, that as I sat reading it in my study, tears fell from my eyes; tears of gratitude. Then, before I realized what I was doing, I rose from my chair and called her name to show it to her—forgetting for a moment that she was gone. You will never know how much your letter has warmed my spirit. I have been walking about in the glow of it all day long.

Need I say anything more? I want you to make a practice of thanking people; of taking a little trouble to thank them. It will please God. He often sends His special mercies by the hands of other people. He *normally* does. I think He likes His agent to be thanked also. Here is a resolution to be made at the time of Harvest Festival. Give thanks! Give Thanks!

3. The Greatest Blessing—Tragically Ignored

First, the common blessings commonly overlooked; secondly, the special blessings soon forgotten; thirdly, *the greatest blessing—tragically ignored.*

What is the greatest blessing? Oh, there is no doubt about that. Paul was quite a master of words and he seldom found that they failed him, but there *was* a subject on which words fell short, and on one occasion, when it came to his mind, he said: "Thanks be to God for His unspeakable gift."

Note that word *unspeakable*. Paul was saying, in effect: "It just won't go into words."

What was so wonderful that it wouldn't go into words? What had the Father given for which no thanks were really adequate?

The gift of Jesus Christ! He was the unspeakable gift. Thanks be to God (above everything else), says Paul for Him.

I have often sat down and meditated on what my life would have been, without Christ. It is a dark picture. Poor as I know my life still to be, I dare hardly think of it apart from Him. When Baron von Hugel considered the same question, he said of the religion of Jesus:

> I should not be physically alive at this moment; I should be, were I alive at all, a corrupt or at least an incredibly unhappy, violent, bitter, self-occupied destructive soul, were it not for religion and for its having come and saved me from myself—it, and nothing else, it, in a sense, against everything else.

All this he felt about the power of Christ in his life. I would phrase it differently, but my own honest witness would be no less emphatic than his. I believe every good thing in my life came from God and—if any doubter wanted to wipe that aside as nothing but an act of faith—I would go farther and say that I can actually *trace* most of them. My deepening conviction that divine love is the only satisfying motive in life, my life's partner, my blissfully happy home, the love of child and friend, the joy of service . . . they all came as smaller gifts in the hand of "the unspeakable Gift"—from Christ Himself.

Nor are the blessings only personal. When I see this dark world through His eyes, I have hope for it. When I feel the pulse of His power remolding my own stubborn nature, I know what He can do with all people. When I see His clear reflection in the saints—in men and women who have given Him the fullest opportunity—I know again that He is the Savior of the world.

Yet multi-millions who know of Him ignore Him, deny His worldwide and all-time significance, assert that this world belongs to us who never called it into being nor understand how it works, spurn the "unspeakable gift" as a figment of our child minds.

Be wiser than they are! At this time of thanksgiving—thanksgiving for the harvest, but much more than the harvest—thank God for His "unspeakable gift" in whose hand every other precious thing comes as well.

One of the worst moments for an atheist is when he feels thankful and has no One to thank! You are not in that position! You thank the Father for the Son and both for the Holy Spirit. To trace every "good and perfect gift" to its true source—the Father of Light—is a good thing; it keeps one orientated to the Highest; it maintains the concept of reverence in our minds without which every mortal mind is deficient; it reminds us who is in charge.

Conclusion

I conclude with this:

We are often rebuked in our thanklessness by people less fortunate than we are ourselves, and we are often reminded by them of the number and source of our blessings.

Here is an instance. A ministerial friend of mine used to visit an invalid girl. She was a devout person. One of her several sicknesses was a tendency to curvature of the spine and she lived in a Phelp's box. Have you ever seen a Phelp's box? It looks like a shallow coffin—a grisly anticipation of the grave—and children with a tendency to curvature of the spine used to be strapped in one, as nearly flat as possible.

Her box was by the window, and she said to my friend one day:

"In this position I can only look up. On those nights when I can't sleep, I play with the stars."

"Play with the stars?" he asked. "How can you play with the stars?"

"This way," she said. "I pick out the brightest star I can find and I say: 'That's Mummy.' I pick out another bright one, and say: 'That's Daddy.' I find a twinkling one for my brother, my puppy, my spinal perambulator . . ." on and on she went. Nothing seemed forgotten. Then she concluded with this:

"But there aren't enough stars to go around!"

There aren't enough stars to go around!

Go home, you thankless people, and count the stars!

NOTES

Praise Thy God, O Zion!

Charles Haddon Spurgeon (1834–1892) is undoubtedly the most famous minister of the last century. Converted in 1850, he united with the Baptists and soon began to preach in various places. He became pastor of the Baptist church in Waterbeach in 1851, and three years later he was called to the decaying Park Street Church, London. Within a short time the work began to prosper, a new church was built and dedicated in 1861, and Spurgeon became London's most popular preacher. In 1855 he began to publish his sermons weekly; and today they make up the fifty-seven volumes of *The Metropolitan Tabernacle Pulpit*. He founded a pastor's college and several orphanages.

This sermon is taken from *The Metropolitan Tabernacle Pulpit*, Volume 12 and was preached on February 25, 1866.

Charles Haddon Spurgeon

10

PRAISE THY GOD, O ZION!

And when he was come nigh, even now at the descent of
the mount of Olives, the whole multitude of the disciples
began to rejoice and praise God with a loud voice for all the
mighty works that they had seen; Saying, Blessed be the
King that cometh in the name of the Lord: peace in heaven,
and glory in the highest. And some of the Pharisees from
among the multitude said unto him, Master, rebuke thy
disciples. And he answered and said unto them, I tell you
that, if these should hold their peace, the stones would
immediately cry out (Luke 19:37–40).

THE SAVIOR WAS "a man of sorrows," but every thoughtful
mind has discovered the fact that down deep in His
innermost soul He must have carried an inexhaustible
treasury of refined and heavenly joy. I suppose that of all
the human race there was never a man who had a deeper,
purer, or more abiding peace than our Lord Jesus Christ.
"He was anointed with the oil of gladness above his
fellows." Benevolence is joy. The highest benevolence must
from the very nature of things have afforded the deepest
possible delight. To be engaged in the most blessed of all
errands, to foresee the marvelous results of His labors in
time and in eternity, and even to see around Him the
fruits of the good which He had done in the healing of the
sick and the raising of the dead must have given to such a
sympathetic heart as that which beat within the bosom of
the Lord Jesus Christ much of secret satisfaction and joy.
There were a few remarkable seasons when this joy
manifested itself. "At that hour Jesus rejoiced in spirit
and said, I thank thee, O Father, Lord of heaven and
earth." Christ had His songs though it was night with
Him; and though His face was marred and His
countenance had lost the luster of earthly happiness, yet
sometimes it was lit up with a matchless splendor of

unparalleled satisfaction as He thought upon the recompense of the reward and in the midst of the congregation sang His praise unto God.

In this, the Lord Jesus is a blessed picture of His church on earth. This is the day of Zion's trouble; at this hour the church expects to walk in sympathy with her Lord along a thorny road. She is without the camp—through much tribulation she is forcing her way to the crown. She expects to meet with reproaches. To bear the cross is her office, and to be scorned and counted an alien by her mother's children is her lot. And yet the church has a deep well of joy, of which none can drink but her own children. There are stores of wine and oil and corn hidden in the midst of our Jerusalem, upon which the saints of God are evermore sustained and nurtured; and sometimes, as in our Savior's case, we have our seasons of intense delight, for "there is a river, the streams whereof make glad the city of our God." Exiles though we be, we rejoice in our King, yea in Him we exceedingly rejoice; while in His name we set up our banners.

This is a season with us as a church when we are peculiarly called upon to rejoice in God. The Lord Jesus, in the narrative before us, was going to Jerusalem, as His disciples fondly hoped, to take the throne of David and set up the long-expected kingdom. Well might they shout for joy, for the Lord was in their midst, in their midst in state, riding amidst the acclamations of a multitude who had been glad partakers of His goodness. Jesus Christ is in our midst today; the kingdom is securely His. We see the crown glittering upon His brow; He has been riding through our streets, healing our blind, raising our dead, and speaking words of comfort to our mourners. We, too, attend Him in state today, and the acclamations of little children are not wanting, for from the Sabbath school there have come songs of converted youngsters, who sing gladly, as did the children of Jerusalem in days of yore, "Hosanna! Blessed is he that cometh in the name of the Lord!"

I want, dear friends, this morning, to stir up in all of us the spirit of holy joy, because our King is in our midst;

that we may welcome Him and rejoice in Him, and that while He is working His mighty deeds of salvation throughout this congregation so graciously, He may not lack such music as our feeble lips can afford Him. I shall therefore invite your attention to these four verses, by way of example, that we may take a pattern for our praise from this inspired description. We shall observe four things: first, *delightful praise*; secondly, *appropriate song*; thirdly, *intrusive objections*; fourthly, *an unanswerable argument*.

1. Delightful Praise

In the thirty-seventh verse every word is significant and deserves the careful notice of all who would learn aright the lesson of how to magnify the Savior. To begin with, the praise rendered to Christ was *speedy praise*. The happy choristers did not wait till He had entered the city, but "when he was come nigh, even now, at the descent of the mount of Olives, they began to rejoice." It is well to have a quick eye to perceive occasions for gratitude. Blind unbelief and blear-eyed thanklessness allow the favors of God to be forgotten in unthankfulness and, without praises, die; they walk in the noonday of mercy and see no light to sing by; but a believing, cheerful, grateful spirit detects at once the rising of the sun of mercy and begins to sing, even at the break of day. Christian, if you would sing of the mercy you have already, you would soon have more. If twilight made you glad, you should soon have the bliss of noon. I am certain that the church in these days has lost much by not being thankful for little. We have had many prayer meetings, but few, very few, praise meetings; as if the church could cry loud enough when her own ends were to be answered but was dumb as to music for her Lord. Her King acts to her very much as He did with the man with the pound. That man put not out the pound to interest, and therefore it was taken away. We have not thanked Him for little mercies, and therefore even these have been removed, and churches have become barren and deserted by the Spirit of God. Let *us* lift up the voice of praise to our Master, because He has blessed us these twelve years. We have had a continual stream of revival. The cries of sinners have sounded in our ears—every day we have seen souls converted—I was about to say almost every hour of the week, and that by the space of these twelve years, and of late, we have had a double portion. Benjamin's mess has been set near our place at the table; we have been made to feast on royal dainties and have been filled with bread even to the full. Shall we not then praise God? Ah! let us not require twice telling of it, but let our souls begin to praise Him, even now that He comes nigh unto Jerusalem.

It strikes us at once, also, that this was *unanimous* praise. Observe, not only the multitude, but the *whole multitude* of the disciples rejoiced and praised Him; not one silent tongue among the disciples—not one who withheld his song. And yet, I suppose, those disciples had their trials as we have ours. There might have been a sick wife at home or a child withering with disease. They were doubtless poor, we know they were, indeed; and poverty is never without its pinches. They were men of like passions with ourselves; they had to struggle with inbred sin and with temptation from without, and yet there seems to have been no one who on those grounds excluded himself from the choir of singers on that happy day. Oh, my soul, whatever thorn about you which might bow you down, be you glad when you remember that Jesus Christ is glorified in the midst of His church. Wherefore, my brother, is that harp of yours hanging on the willows? Have you nothing to sing about? Has He done nothing for you? Why, if you have no personal reason for blessing God, then lend us your heart and voice to help us, for we have more praise work on hand than we can get through alone—we have more to praise Him for than we are able to discharge without extra aid. Our work of praise is too great for us, come and help us; sing on our behalf if you cannot on your own; and then, mayhap, you will catch the flame and find something after all for which you, too, must bless Him.

I know there are some of you who do not feel as if you could praise God this morning; let us ask the Master to put your harp in tune. Oh be not silent! Be not silent! Do bless Him! If you cannot bless Him for temporals, do bless Him for spirituals; and if you have not of late experimentally enjoyed many of these, then bless Him for what He is. For that dear face, covered with the bloody sweat; for those pierced hands, for that opened side, will you not praise Him? Why, surely, if He had not died for me, yet I must love Him to think of His goodness in dying for others. His kindness, the generosity of His noble heart in dying for His enemies might well provoke the most unbelieving to a song. I am, therefore, not content unless all of you will contribute your note. I would have every bird throw in its note, though some cannot imitate the lark or nightingale; yea, I would have every tree of the forest clap its hands, and even the hyssop on the wall wave in adoration. Come, beloved, cheer up. Let dull care and dark fear be gone. Up with harps and down with doubts. It must be praise from "the whole multitude." The praise must be unanimous—not one chord out of order to spoil the tune.

Next, it was *multitudinous*. "The whole multitude." There is something most inspiriting and exhilarating in the noise of a multitude singing God's praises. Sometimes, when we have been in good tune and have sung "Praise God from whom all blessings flow," our music has rolled upward like thunder to yon dome and has reverberated peal on peal, and these have been the happiest moments some of us have ever known, when every tongue was praise, and every heart was joy. Oh, let us renew those happy times; let us anticipate the season when the dwellers in the east and in the west, in the north and in the south, of every age and of every clime, shall assemble on the celestial hilltops and swell the everlasting song, extolling Jesus Lord of all. Jesus loves the praise of many; He loves to hear the voices of all the blood-washed.

> Ten thousand thousand are their tongues,
> But all their joys are one.

We are not so many as that, but we are counted by thousands, and let us praise His name—the whole multitude.

Still it is worthy of observation that, while the praise was multitudinous, it was quite *select*. It was the whole multitude *of the disciples*. The Pharisees did not praise Him—they were murmuring. All true praise must come from true hearts. If you do not learn of Christ, you cannot render to Him acceptable song. These disciples, of course, were of different sorts. Some of them had but just enlisted in the army—just learned to sit at His feet. Some had worked miracles in His name and, having been called to the apostolic office, had preached the word to others; but they were all disciples. I trust that in this congregation there is a vast majority of disciples; well, then, all of you, you who have lately come into His school, you who have long been in it, you who have become fathers in Israel and are teaching others, the whole multitude of disciples, I hope, will praise God. I could wish—God grant the wish—I could wish that those who are not disciples might soon become so. "Take my yoke upon you," said He, "and learn of me, for I am meek and lowly in heart." A disciple is a learner. You may not know much, but you need not know anything in coming to Christ. Christ begins with ignorance and bestows wisdom. If you do but know that you know nothing, you know enough to become a disciple of Christ Jesus. There is no matriculation necessary in order to enter into Christ's college. He takes the fools and makes them know the wonders of His dying love. Oh that you may become a disciple! "Write my name down, sir," say you to the writer with the inkhorn by his side, and be henceforth a humble follower of the Lamb. Now, though I would not have those who are not disciples close their mouths when ever others sing, yet I do think there are some hymns in which they would behave more honestly if they did not join, for there are some expressions which hardly ought to come from unconverted lips; better far would it be if they would pray, "Lord, open thou my lips, and my mouth shall shew forth thy praise." You may have a very sweet voice, my friend, and may sing with admirable taste and in exquisite harmony any of the parts, but God does not accept the praise where the heart is absent. The best tune in the book is one called *Hearts*.

The whole multitude of the disciples whom Jesus loves are the proper persons to extol the Redeemer's name. May you, dear hearer, be among that company!

Then, in the next place, you will observe that the praise they rendered was *joyful praise.* "The whole multitude of the disciples began to rejoice." I hope the doctrine that Christians ought to be gloomy will soon be driven out of the universe. There are no people in the world who have such a right to be happy nor have such cause to be joyful as the saints of the living God. All Christian duties should be done joyfully, but especially the work of praising the Lord. I have been in congregations where the tune was dolorous to the very last degree; where the time was so dreadfully slow that one wondered whether they would ever be able to sing through the Psalm 119; whether, to use Watts' expression, eternity would not be too short for them to get through it; and altogether, the spirit of the people has seemed to be so damp, so heavy, so dead, that we might have supposed that they were met to prepare their minds for hanging rather than for blessing the ever-gracious God. Why, brethren, true praise sets the heart ringing its bells and hanging out its streamers. Never hang your flag at half-mast when you praise God; no, run up every color, let every banner wave in the breeze, and let all the powers and passions of your spirit exult and rejoice in God your Savior. They *rejoiced.* We are really most horribly afraid of being too happy. Some Christians think cheerfulness a very dangerous folly, if not a ruinous vice. That joyous Psalm 100 has been altered in all the English versions.

> All people that on earth do dwell,
> Sing to the Lord with cheerful voice,
> Him serve with fear, his praise forth tell,
> Come ye before him and rejoice.

"Him serve with fear," says the English version; but the Scotch version has less thistle and far more rose in it. Listen to it, and catch its holy happiness:

> Him serve with *mirth*, his praise forth tell;
> Come ye before him and rejoice.

How do God's creatures serve Him out of doors? The birds do not sit on a Sunday with folded wings, dolefully silent on the boughs of the trees, but they sing as sweetly as may be, even though the raindrops fall. As for the new born lambs in the field—they skip to His praise, though the season is damp and cold. Heaven and earth are lit up with gladness, and why not the hearts and houses of the saints? "Him serve with mirth." Well said the psalmist: "before him exceedingly rejoice." It was *joyful* praise.

The next point we must mention is that it was *demonstrative* praise. They praised Him with their voices and with a loud voice. Propriety very greatly objects to the praise which is rendered by Primitive Methodists at times; their shouts and hallelujahs are thought by some delicate minds to be very shocking. I would not, however, join in the censure, lest I should be numbered among the Pharisees who said, "Master, rebuke thy disciples." I wish more people were as earnest and even as vehement as the Methodists used to be. In our Lord's day we see that the people expressed the joy which they felt; I am not sure that they expressed it in the most tunable manner, but at any rate they expressed it in a hearty, lusty shout. They altogether praised with a *loud* voice. It is said of Mr. Rowland Hill that, on one occasion, someone sat on the pulpit stairs, who sang in his ears with such a sharp shrill voice, that he could endure it no longer, but said to the good woman, "I wish you would be quiet"; when she answered, "It comes from my heart." "Oh," said he, "pray forgive me—sing away: sing as loudly as you will." And truly, dear friends, though one might wish there were more melody in it, yet if your music comes from the heart, we cannot object to the loudness, or we might be found objecting to that which the Savior could not and would not blame. Must we not be loud? Do you wonder that we speak out? Have not His mercies a loud tongue? Do not His kindnesses deserve to be proclaimed aloud? Were not the cries upon the cross so loud that the very rocks were rent thereby, and shall our music be a whisper? No, as Watts declares, we would—

Loud as his thunders shout his praise,
And sound it lofty as his throne.

If not with loud voices actually in sound, yet we would make the praise of God loud by our actions, which speak louder than any words; we would extol Him by great deeds of kindness and love and self-denial and zeal, that so our actions may assist our words. "The whole multitude praised him with a loud voice." Let me ask every Christian here to do something in the praise of God, to speak in some way for his Master. I would say, speak today; if you cannot with your voice, speak by act and deed; but do join in the hearty shout of all the saints of God while you praise and bless the name of our ever-gracious Lord.

The praise rendered, however, though very demonstrative, was very *reasonable*; the reason is given—"for all the mighty works that they had seen." My dear friends, we have seen many mighty works which Christ has done. I do not know what these disciples had happened to see. Certain it is, that after Christ entered into Jerusalem, He was lavish of His miracles. The blind were healed, the deaf had their ears opened, many of those possessed with devils were delivered, and incurable diseases gave way at His word. I think we have the like reason in a spiritual sense. What has God wrought? It has been marvelous— as our elders would tell you, if they could recount what God has done—the many who have come forward during the last fortnight to tell what God has done for their souls. The Holy Spirit has met with some whom hitherto no ministry had reached. Some have been convinced of sin who were wrapped up in self-righteous rags; others have been comforted whose desponding hearts drew nigh unto despair. I am sure those brethren who sat to see inquirers must have been astonished when they found some hundreds coming to talk about the things that make for their peace. It was blessed work, I doubt not, for them. They, therefore, would lead the strain. But you have all in your measure seen something of it. During the meetings we have held we have enjoyed an overpowering sense of the Divine presence. Without excitement there has been a holy humility of spirit and yet a blessed lifting up of hope and joy and holy fervor. The Master has cast sweet smiles upon His church; He has come near to His beloved; He has given her the tokens of His affection and made her to rejoice with joy unspeakable. Any joy which we have toward Christ, then, will be reasonable enough, for we have seen His mighty works.

With another remark, I shall close this first head—the reason for their joy was a *personal* one. There is no praise to God so sweet as that which flows from the man or woman who has tasted that the Lord is gracious. Some of you have been converted during the last two or three months. Oh! you *must* bless Him, you *shall*; you must take the front rank now and bless His name for the mighty work which you have seen in yourself. The things which once were dear to you you now abhor, and those things which seemed dry and empty are now sweet and full of savor. God has turned your darkness into light. He has brought you up out of the horrible pit and out of the miry clay and has set your feet upon a rock; shall not your established goings yield Him a grateful song? You shall bless Him. Others here present have had their own children saved. God has looked on one family and another and taken one, and two, and three. He has been pleased to lay His hand upon the elders among us and bless their families. Oh sing unto His name! Sing praises for the mighty works which we have seen.

This will be common-place talk enough to those of you who have not seen it; but those who have will feel the tears starting to their eyes as they think of son and daughter, of whom they can say, "Behold, he prays." Saints of God I wish I could snatch a firebrand from the altar of praise that burns before the great throne of God: I wish I could fire your hearts therewith, but it is the Master's work to do it. Oh! may He do it now. May every one of you feel as if you could cast your crown at His feet; as if you could sing like the cherubim and the seraphim nor yield even the first place of gratitude to the brightest spirit before the eternal throne. This morning may it be truly said, "The whole multitude of

the disciples rejoiced with a loud voice for all the mighty
things which they had seen."

> O come, loud anthems let us sing
> Loud thanks to our Almighty King;
> For we our voices high should raise,
> When our salvation's rock we praise.
>
> Into his presence let us haste,
> To thank him for his favors past;
> To him address, in joyful songs,
> The praise that to His name belongs.

2. An Appropriate Song

I shall now lead you on to the second point—their praise
found vent for itself in *an appropriate song*. "Blessed be
the King that cometh in the name of the Lord. Peace in
heaven, and glory in the highest."

It was an appropriate song, if you will remember that
it had Christ for its subject. "My heart is indicting of a
good matter: I speak of the things which I have made
touching the king." No song is so sweet from believing lips
as that which tells of Him who loved us and who gave
Himself for us. This particular song sings of Christ in His
character of King—a right royal song then—a melody fit
for a coronation day. Crown Him! Crown Him Lord of all!
That was the refrain—"Blessed be the King." It sang of
that King as commissioned by the Most High, "who cometh
in the name of the Lord." To think of Christ as bearing
divine authority, as coming down to humanity in God our
Father's name, speaking what He has heard in heaven,
fulfilling no self-espoused errand but a mission upon which
the Divine Father sent Him according to His purpose and
decree; all this is matter for music. Oh bless the Lord,
saints, as you remember that your Savior is the Lord's
Anointed. He has set Him on His throne; He Jehovah,
who was pleased to bruise Him, has said, "Yet have I set
my King upon my holy hill of Zion." See the Godhead of
your Savior. He whom you adore, the Son of Mary, is the
Son of God. He who did ride upon a colt the foal of an ass
did also ride upon a cherub and did fly; yea, He rode upon

the wings of the wind. They spread their garments in the way and brake down branches; it was a humble triumph, but long ere this the angels had strewn His path with adoring songs. Before Him went the lightnings, coals of fire were in His track, and up from His throne went forth hailstones and coals of fire. Blessed be the King! Oh praise Him this day; praise the King, divine, and commissioned of His Father. The burden of their song was, however, of Christ *present in their midst*. I do not think they would have rejoiced so loudly and sweetly if *He* had not been there. That was the source and center of their mirth—the King riding upon a colt the foal of an ass—the King triumphant. They could not but be glad when He revealed Himself. Beloved, our King is here. We sang at the beginning of this visitation, "Arise, O King of grace, arise, and enter to thy rest!" You remember our singing the verse—

> O thou that art the Mighty One,
> Thy sword gird on thy thigh.

And King Jesus has done so in state; He has ridden prosperously, and out of the ivory palaces His heart has been made glad; and the King's daughter, all-glorious within, standing at His right hand, cannot but be glad too. Loud to His praise wake every string of your heart, and let your souls make the Lord Jesus the burden of your song.

This was an appropriate song, in the next place, because *it had God for its object*; they extolled God, God in Christ, when they thus lifted up their voices. They said, "Peace in heaven, and glory in the highest." When we extol Christ, we desire to bless the infinite majesty that gave Christ to us. Thanks be unto the Father for His unspeakable gift. O eternal God, we Your creatures in this little world do unfeignedly bless You for that great purpose and decree, by which You did choose us to be illustrious exhibitions of Your majesty and love. We bless You that You did give us grace in Christ Your Son before the starry sky was spread abroad. We praise thee, O God, and magnify Your name as we inquire, "What is man, that thou art mindful of him, or the son of man, that thou visitest him?" How could You deign to stoop from all the glory of Your infinity, to be made man, to suffer, to bleed, to die for us? "Give unto the Lord, O ye mighty, give unto the Lord glory and strength. Give unto the Lord the glory that is due unto his name." Oh that I could give place to some inspired bard, some seer of old, who standing before you with mouth streaming with holy eloquence, should extol Him that lives but once was slain and bless the God who sent Him here below that He might redeem to Himself a people who should show forth His praise.

I think this song to have been very appropriate for another reason, namely, because *it had the universe for its scope.* It was not praise within walls as ours this morning; the multitude sung in the open air with no walls but the horizon, with no roof but the unpillared arch of heaven. Their song, though it was from heaven, did not stay there but enclosed the world within its range. It was, "Peace in heaven; glory in the highest." It is very singularly like that song of the angels, that Christmas carol of the spirits from on high when Christ was born; but it differs, for the angels' song was, "Peace on earth," and this at the gates of Jerusalem was, "Peace in heaven." It is the nature of song to spread itself. From heaven the sacred joy began when angels sang, and then the fire blazed down to earth in the words, "Peace on earth"; but now the song began on earth, and so it blazed up to heaven with the words, "Peace in heaven: glory in the highest." Is not it a wonderful thing that a company of poor beings, like us here below, can really affect the highest heavens? Every throb of gratitude which heaves in our hearts glows through heaven. God can receive no actual increase of glory from His creature, for He has infinite glory and majesty, but yet the creature manifests that glory. A grateful man here below, when his heart is all on fire with sacred love, warms heaven itself. The multitude sung of peace in heaven, as though the angels were established in their peaceful seats by the Savior, as though the war which God had waged with sin was over now, because the conquering King was come. Oh let us seek after music which shall be fitted for other spheres! I would begin the music here, and so my soul should rise. Oh for some heavenly notes to bear my passions to the skies! It was appropriate to the occasion, because the universe was its sphere.

And it seems also to have been most appropriate, because it had *gratitude for its spirit.* They cried aloud, *Blessed*—"Blessed be the King." We cannot bless God in the sense in which He blesses us, and yet we do bless Him. Our goodness cannot extend to Him, but we reflect the blessedness which streams from Him as light from the sun. Blessed be Jesus! My brethren, have you never wished to make Him happier? Have you not wished that you could extol Him? Let Him be exalted! Let Him sit on high! I have almost wished even selfishly that He were not so glorious as He is, that we might help to lift Him higher. Oh! if the crushing of my body, soul, and spirit would make Him one atom more glorious, I would not only consent to the sacrifice, but bless His name that He counted me worthy so to do. All that we can do brings nothing unto Him. Yet, brethren, I would that He had His own. Oh that He rode over our great land in triumph! Would that King Jesus were as well known here now as He was once in puritanic times! Would that Scotland were as loyal to Him as in covenanting periods! Would that Jesus had His majesty visible in the eyes of all! We pray for this, we seek for this; and among the chief joys our chiefest joy is to know that God has highly exalted Him and given Him a name which is above every name, that at the name of Jesus every knee should bow. We have thus said something about the appropriateness of the song; may you, each of you, light upon such hymns as will serve to set forth your own case and show forth the mercy of God in saving you, and do not be slack in praising Him in such notes as may be most suitable to your own condition.

3. Intrusive Objections

Thirdly, and very briefly—for I am not going to give much time to these men—we have *intrusive objections.* "Master, rebuke thy disciples." We know that voice—the old grunt of the Pharisee. What could he do otherwise?

Such is the man, and such must his communications be. While he can dare to boast, "God, I thank thee that I am not as other men are," he is not likely to join in praises such as other men lift up to heaven.

But why did these Pharisees object? I suppose it was first of all because *they thought there would be no praise for them.* If the multitude had been saying, "Oh these *blessed* Pharisees! these excellent Pharisees! What broad phylacteries! What admirable hems to their garments! How diligently and scrupulously they tithe their mint and their anise and their cumin! What a wonder that God should permit us poor vile creatures to look upon these super-excellent incarnations of virtue!" I will be bound to say there would not have been a man among them who would have said, "Master, rebuke thy disciples." A proud heart never praises God, for it hoards up praise for itself.

In the next place, *they were jealous of the people.* They did not feel so happy themselves, and they could not bear that other people should be glad. They were like the elder brother who said, "Yet thou never gavest me a kid, that I might make merry with my friends." Was that a reason why nobody else should be merry? A very ill reason truly! Oh, if we cannot rejoice ourselves, let us stand out of the way of other people. If we have no music in our own hearts, let us not wish to stop those who have.

But I think the main point was that they were *jealous of Jesus;* they did not like to have Christ crowned with majesty. Certainly this is the drift of the human heart. It does not wish to see Jesus Christ extolled. Preach up morality or dry doctrine or ceremonies, and many will be glad to hear your notes; but preach up Jesus Christ, and some will say, "Master, rebuke thy disciples!" It was not ill advice of an old preacher to a young beginner, when he said, "Preach nothing down but sin, and preach nothing up but Christ." Brethren, let us praise nothing up but Christ. Have nothing to say about your church, say nothing about your denomination, hold your tongue about the minister, but praise Christ, and I know the Pharisees will not like it, but that is an excellent reason to give them more of it, for that which Satan does not admire, he ought to have more of. The preaching of Christ is the whip that flogs the devil; the preaching of Christ is the thunderbolt, the sound of which makes all hell shake. Let us never be silent then; we shall put to confusion all our foes, if we do but extol Christ Jesus the Lord. "Master, rebuke thy disciples!" Well, there is not much of this for Jesus Christ to rebuke in the Christian Church in the present day. There used to be—there used to be a little of what the world calls fanaticism. A consecrated cobbler once set forth to preach the gospel in Hindustan. There were men who would go preaching the gospel among the heathen, counting not their lives dear unto them. The day was when the church was so foolish as to fling away precious lives for Christ's glory. Ah! she is more prudent now-a-days. Alas! alas! for your prudence. She is so calm and so quiet—no Methodist's zeal now—even that denomination which did seem alive has become most proper and most cold. And we are so charitable too. We let the most abominable doctrines be preached, and we put our finger on our lip, and say, "There's so many good people who think so." Nothing is to be rebuked now-a-days. Brethren, one's soul is sick of this! Oh, for the old fire again! The church will never prosper till it comes once more. Oh, for the old fanaticism, for that indeed was the Spirit of God making men's spirits in earnest! Oh, for the old doing and daring that risked everything and cared for nothing, except to glorify Him who shed His blood upon the cross! May we live to see such bright and holy days again! The world may murmur, but Christ will not rebuke.

4. An Unanswerable Argument

We come now to the last point, which is this—*an unanswerable argument*. He said, "If these should hold their peace, the very stones would cry out."

Brethren, I think that is very much our case; if we were not to praise God, the very stones might cry out against us. We *must* praise the Lord. Woe is unto us if we do not! It is impossible for us to hold our tongues. Saved from hell and be silent! Secure of heaven and be ungrateful! Bought with precious blood and hold our tongues!

Filled with the Spirit and not speak! Restrain, from fear of feeble man, the Spirit's course within our souls! God forbid. In the name of the Most High, let such a thought be given to the winds. What, our children saved; the off-spring of our loins brought to Christ! What, see them springing up like willows by the water courses, and no awakening of song, no gladness, no delight! Oh, then we were worse than brutes, and our hearts would have been steeled and become as adamant. We must praise God! What, the King in our midst, King Jesus smiling into our souls, feasting us at His table, making His Word precious to us, and not praise Him! Why if Satan could know the delight of Christ's company he might begin to love; but we, we were worse than devils if we did not praise the name of Jesus! What! the King's arm made bare, His enemies subdued, His triumphant chariot rolling through our streets, and no song! Oh Zion, if we forget to sing let our right hand forget her cunning, if we count not the King's triumph above our chiefest joy. What, the King coming! His advent drawing nigh, the signs of blessing in the sky and air around, and yet no song! Oh, we must bless Him! Hosanna! Blessed is He that comes in the name of the Lord!

But could the stones ever cry out? Yes, that they could, and if they were to speak they would have much to talk of even as we have this day. If the stones were to speak they could tell of their *Maker*; and shall not we tell of Him who made us anew and out of stones raised up children unto Abraham? They could speak of ages long since gone; the old rocks could tell of chaos and order and the handiwork of God in various stages of creation's drama; and cannot we talk of God's decrees, of God's great work in ancient times, and all that He did for His church? If the stones were to speak they could tell of their *breaker*, how He took them from the quarry and made them fit for the temple; and cannot we tell of our Creator and Maker, who broke our hearts with the hammer of His Word that He might build us into His temple? If the stones were to speak, they would tell of their *builder*, who polished them and fashioned them after the similitude of a palace; and shall not we talk of our Architect and Builder, who has put us in our place in the temple of the living God? Oh, if the stones could speak, they might have a long, long story to tell by way of *memorial*, for many a time has a great stone been rolled as a memorial unto God; and we can tell of Ebenezers, stones of help, stones of remembrance. The broken stones of the Law cry out against us, but Christ Himself, who has rolled away the stone from the door of the sepulcher, speaks for us. Stones might well cry out, but we will not let them; we will hush their noise with ours; we will break forth into sacred song and bless the majesty of the Most High all our days. Let this day and tomorrow be especially consecrated to holy joys, and may the Lord in infinite mercy fill your souls right full of it, both in practical deeds of kindness and benevolence and works of praise! Blessed be His name who lives forever and ever!

NOTES

Grace and Gratitude

James S. Stewart (1896–1990) pastored three churches
in Scotland before becoming professor of theology at the
University of Edinburgh (1936) and then professor of New
Testament (1946). But he was a professor who preached,
a scholar who applied biblical truth to the needs of common
people, and a theologian who made doctrine practical and
exciting. He published several books of lectures and biblical
studies including *A Man in Christ* and *Heralds of God*.
His two finest books of sermons are *The Gates of New Life*
and *The Strong Name*.

This sermon is taken from *The Wind of the Spirit*,
published in 1968 by Abingdon Press.

James S. Stewart

11

GRACE AND GRATITUDE

Were there not ten cleansed? but where are the nine? (Luke 17:17).

THE FIRST THING that strikes you, reading this vivid story, is the dreadful aggregation of trouble on that Jerusalem road. An earlier chapter describes a solitary leper accosting Jesus as He passed. But here is the tragic sight tenfold multiplied, a whole colony of misery, an accumulated horror that might have stunned the heart of Christ Himself.

This is what may well daunt any thinking person looking out at the world today—the mass of trouble there. We have our "Christian Aid" schemes: but, we wonder, can they even begin to cope with the world's accumulated ills? Refugees by the million, starving children, war and famine, crime and delinquency, poverty and ignorance, suffering heaped on suffering, till the imagination staggers and the mind is dazed, and people say—"It does not bear thinking of, it is quite out of hand. No one can possibly deal with it, not governments, not churches, perhaps not even God."

Well, it is not for nothing that St. Luke has shown us the divine omnipotence in action, not only with the individual sufferer, but with this tenfold dilemma.

The Majesty of the Master

There is always a danger that we should be so stunned with the mass of misery that we forget the majesty of the Master, so bewildered by the vastness of the human problem that we overlook the hugeness of the divine resource.

This is where the writers of the New Testament correct us. Not that they minimize the colossal sufferings and tragedies of life. On the contrary. With St. John they say frankly, "The whole world lieth in the Evil One"; with St. Paul, "The whole creation groans, travails in pain." That is there, quite realistically. But this also these men have seen, and this they ring out as the basic elemental fact: there is simply no limit to God's power to break through transformingly into any situation, and no end to the revolutionizing grace of Christ.

What follows? This at the least: whoever may despair of the world, we Christians never can. Do you remember what Rudyard Kipling said about the power of a mother's love to transcend all known limits?

> If I were hanged on the highest hill,
> I know whose love would follow me still.
> If I were drowned in the deepest sea,
> I know whose tears would come down to me.
> If I were damned of body and soul,
> I know whose prayers would make me whole.

If a mother's love can work such miracles, who can possibly limit the love of God Almighty? If only we would give Him faith—not the usual diluted mixture as before of half-belief and doubt and apathy, but a strong simple faith that really took Him at His word—He would corroborate it beyond our dreams. "Lord, I believe; help Thou mine unbelief."

Let us come back to the ten lepers on the road. "They lifted up their voices and cried, Jesus, Master, have mercy on us." That at least was a rudimentary faith. The whole leper fraternity had heard by this time of Christ's cure of one of their own number. And now—"It happened to him," these ten were thinking, "then perhaps there is hope for anyone. Why not for us?" And they determined to put it to the test. "Jesus, Master, have mercy!"

Note Jesus' reply: "Go, show yourselves to the priests." Why that? The reason is clear. For the priests, as Leviticus indicates, were also the Medical Officers of Health. Medicine and religion were much more closely integrated then than now. If you had recovered from some infectious ailment involving quarantine and isolation, you would apply to the priest—the local Medical Officer of Health—for the necessary health certificate.

What is strange in the story is that Jesus apparently said this before any cure had happened. That, to say the least of it, was unusual.

But at any rate they had faith enough to obey. Certainly they could have refused. They might have stood looking at Jesus in blank astonishment. "Go to the priests? And pray, what is the use of that with our disease upon us still? Why such a fruitless journey?" But no. There was something in Jesus' tones, something in those magnetic eyes, that compelled obedience.

They started off to the priests. And somewhere along that road, says the evangelist, the wonderful thing happened—the torpor and numbness passing away, the flagging strength renewed: "it came to pass, as they went they were cleansed." As they obeyed Christ's plain command, the longed for healing came.

Getting on the Road

This is so often the way of it still. The great things the Christian religion talks of—life and healing, the integration of personality, the ending of the sense of meaninglessness and anxiety and boredom, the gift of hope and courage, vitality and joy, everything in fact that the Bible means by "salvation"—these things do not come by sitting down and dreaming of them or by theorizing about their possibility. They do not even come by staying on your knees indefinitely and praying for them. They do come by practical experimentation, by getting your feet on to the road of ethical obedience in simple day to day loyalty. I fancy some of us—even if we cannot see the distant scene—at least know the next step we are meant to take, the plain unspectacular obedience God is asking from us at this moment. That is the way to the miracle. "As they went, they were cleansed."

Let us try to imagine it now, as it might have been, here in St. Luke's narrative. A mile or two down the road, that thrilling indescribable moment when they realized their healing—the sudden surge of gratitude, ten voices praising God for Christ the great Physician—"We are clean! O blessed Healer! We must go back and thank

Him. Let us retrace our steps without delay and find Him. For out of the depths we cried, and God heard us; out of the darkness of hell, and He has answered us. Come, let us fling ourselves in worship at His feet." And so back they come, all ten of them, chanting their tenfold psalm until, yonder is Jesus, and they run to Him and fall down before Him, crying "Blessed Jesus! Heaven-sent Physician! Thanks be to God!"

But no. That is not the story. That is not what the evangelist has to tell. One came back. The rest—ninety percent—are never heard of again.

What is our reaction? Probably to say—"What a pitiable revelation of human nature! What atrocious ingratitude, rank bad manners and discourtesy! Surely this is quite untypical. It is not how people act." Is that how we feel?

More Ready to Pray Than to Praise

Well, we are wrong. This is not untypical in the least. These nine men were more ready to pray than to praise, more ready with petition than with thanksgiving. "Jesus, have mercy on us." That is there in the story all right, but not "Praise, my soul, the King of heaven!"

Is that so untypical? What about ourselves? We are ready enough to run to God with our petitions, ready when things are going badly to burst in on the mercy-seat clamoring hotly—"Lord, it is not fair! The world is grossly mismanaged, and can't You do something about it?" So petition outruns gratitude. "I'll think more of your prayers," wrote R. L. Stevenson to one who was somewhat querulous in his religion, "when I see more of your praises!" For "basically and radically," as Karl Barth has declared, "all sin is simply ingratitude."

We are ungrateful creatures often. Think, for instance, of the heaped-up blessings of each returning day. Are we grateful enough for these? There is an excited psalmist who bursts in upon us crying "Blessed be God who daily loadeth us with benefits"—He does not dole them out with stinting hand, but extravagantly loads us with them— this wonderful earth, and the miracle of being alive, and food and shelter, and love and memory and hope, and day and night, and summer and winter. There is just no end to it, cries the psalmist: "He daily loadeth us with benefits. Blessed be God!" But we? We tend to accept it as our due, the bare minimum we have a right to expect, just common mercies.

We had best take care how we use that word *common*. G. K. Chesterton in one place grows positively wrathful with Wordsworth. It is where the poet speaks of "the light of common day." Don't you dare call it common, cries Chesterton in effect, that's blasphemous! "What God hath cleansed, that call not thou common," said the angel to Peter. We love to sing, in the Twenty-third Psalm,

> Goodness and mercy all my life
> Shall surely follow me.

Perhaps we sing it all too easily. Do we realize that if God were to withdraw His goodness and mercy for one day, one hour, one moment even, we could not live? "Everything's grace," cries one of Stevenson's characters in *The Ebb Tide*, "we walk upon it, we breathe it, we live and die by it, it makes the nails and axles of the universe!" Indeed, we are not nearly grateful enough for the mercies of every ordinary day.

And beyond this, what about the signal deliverances we have known, the miraculous answers to prayer, the dramatic interpositions of a loving providence—are we grateful enough for these? "O God," we prayed in the hour of darkness and the nightmare of anxiety, "if You will help me now and here, now 'while the nearer waters roll, while the tempest still is high,' if You will stand by me and bring me through, I will serve You with my life forever." And God did help us, brought us through most wonderfully; but that vow we made, where is it today? Forgotten.

Still further, beyond the daily mercies and the dramatic deliverances, what about the stupendous facts of our historic faith are we grateful enough for these? For God's mighty acts in our redemption? Take the basic statements: "God was made manifest in the flesh. He bore our sins in His own body on the tree. He is risen. He has abolished death. All things are yours, and you are Christ's, and

Christ is God's." As Christians, we accept that. But—are we astonished by it? Are we thrilled? Has it ever overwhelmed us, blinded our eyes with tears of gratitude?

I wonder if those nine who went their way are so very untypical after all?

Let us follow this a stage further. Suppose we ask: Why did they not return to give thanks? Perhaps they felt that they deserved the miracle, that the health given back to them was no more than their human right. "If there is a God in heaven," they felt, "He should never have allowed us to suffer as we have done all these bitter years. And if He has now thought better and removed it, are we to thank Him for such a tardy act of justice? For restoring what should never have been taken away?"

Perhaps that was their feeling. For human nature, even today, even in us, is always tending to claim that it deserves "my rights"—things which are God's sheer grace. Have I deserved my health, when the hospitals of the world are full of sufferers? Have I deserved the human love and affection which have cheered me on my way? Have I deserved to be born into a Christian land of freedom? Have I deserved the miracle of divine forgiveness which has been my salvation? If I know anything at all, it is this, that not one of these gifts have I deserved; they are all the unmerited grace of heaven. In fact, that is what the word *grace* means: something completely and forever undeserved. It is a humbling thought indeed.

Christ Can Wait

That may have been why the lepers failed to return to give thanks: they felt they deserved the miracle. Or perhaps it was not that, but this: other things were more pressing—Christ could wait. There were such urgent matters to be settled. After all, they had been segregated, ostracized, quarantined all these years. Would anyone want them now? Would there be a place waiting for them, when they returned to claim it? Would there be any offer of employment, any work to do? These were the questions they had to get answered; Christ could wait. And in the event, He waited so long that He was quite forgotten.

"Where is He now? We don't know. Where was He going? We forgot to ask. What shall we give Him? We had not thought of that." That may have been the way of it. It is often the way of it today. We do not mean to be ungrateful or irreligious, but—well, look at life—it is not our fault, is it, if we are preoccupied, too burdened with multifarious tasks to have much time for things unseen, too inextricably involved in life's hectic rush to think of going to God and giving Him our love? Who was that knocking at the door? Christ? Oh, that's all right. Christ can wait!

So we find reasons why they did not return. We have rationalized our own attitudes in the same ways often. But what did Jesus think about it? Listen to this poignant word that has rung down the centuries. "Were there not ten cleansed, but where are the nine?" That cry still echoes through the crowded ways of our modern world, right into our own streets and homes today. Where are the nine? Were there not ten houses in that street, and one was glad when the Lord's Day came and the bells called to worship—but where are the nine? Were there not ten blessings the love of heaven heaped upon that life, and one has taken root and borne some harvest—but where are the nine? Were there not ten deliverances wrought for that man, and one has stayed in memory—but where are the nine? Were there not ten secret messages that stirred his conscience, and one has not quite gone with the wind—but where are the nine? "O Jerusalem, Jerusalem," cried Jesus once, "how often would I, and ye would not!" That hurts Christ, really wounds Him.

> Blow, blow, thou winter wind,
> Thou art not so unkind
> As man's ingratitude—

to God! In Christina Rossetti's passionate outcry: "Earth, earth, earth, thy cold is keen!" "I am come," declared our Lord, "to send fire upon the earth. But oh, how slow it is to kindle!"

So here in the story the general mood was "Christ can wait." But there was one man who said, "No—Christ shan't wait! The priests, they can wait. My chance of a job, my place in the world, can wait. But not Christ! Not the grace and love that saved me! And if you nine will not come back with me this moment and find Him and offer yourselves as His disciples, it is rank treason. Christ shan't wait—not the blessed Healer to whom I owe it all!" One came back to tell his gratitude. "I love the Lord, because He hath heard my voice and my supplications. Because He hath inclined His ear unto me, therefore will I call upon Him as long as I live."

His way of telling it was significant. He fell down on his face at Jesus' feet and "with a loud voice glorified God." Perhaps it was not really necessary to be so demonstrative. He could presumably have done it more unostentatiously. He did not need to startle the echoes with his loud doxologies. We don't like those vulgar hallelujahs. Well, that is our loss, not his. This was a man redeemed; why should he not glorify God with a loud voice—not with the diffident apologetic murmur that is sometimes all we can muster, as though it were not quite seemly to make a joyful noise to the Lord, not quite cultured to be too deeply moved even by the love of Christ? This man had no such illogical inhibitions. There was another day when some good religious folk said to Jesus—"Master, rebuke your disciples. Check those unseemly Hosannas!" Swift as an arrow came the reply, "If these should hold their peace, the stones would immediately cry out!" And if I have no heart to praise Him after all He has done for me, the very stones of the street might well find tongue and shout the praises I have failed to render. "With a loud voice he glorified God."

"And he was a Samaritan." That Luke doubly underlines. A Samaritan—that is to say, an outsider, an alien from the Israel of God. In fact, when he turned in his tracks to go back to Christ, I fancy the other nine all said "Let him go: we are better without him. He is not of our class, not even a Jew, a half-breed, a miserable Samaritan!"

Is it not extraordinary how often the unlikeliest folk are the first to respond to Jesus? Our Lord Himself comments on it here: "They are not found who returned to give glory

to God, except this stranger." In Africa, there is a leper
colony where two thousand turn out for the weekly prayer
meeting. Two thousand! And we are glad if we can get
twenty. "Except this stranger." That is the way of it so
often. In Jericho there were any number of worthy religious people; why had it to be a Zacchaeus, that more
than dubious character, who took Jesus home to dinner?
Why had it to be a woman off the streets who anointed
Him for His death and burial? Why had it to be twelve
rough, uncouth fishermen and others to form the nucleus
of a world religion?

> God moves in a mysterious way
> His wonders to perform.

And Christ calls the strangest, unlikeliest folk to be His
helpers and disciples. That is important. It means, you
see, there is some chance for us.

Our Devotion Can Cheer the Soul of Christ

So let us end our study today, not with the indifference
of the nine, but with the gratitude of the one. If that
ninefold apathy hurt Jesus terribly, just see how this one
man's devotion cheered and gladdened Him. It was a lone-
some world for Jesus then, cold, critical, hostile, so that
real loyalty, when He did come upon it, was something
that touched and moved and strengthened Him—just as
the angel, we are told, strengthened Him in Gethsemane.

I put this question to you now, as I put it to my own
soul. Do we realize that our poor stumbling words of devotion can cheer the soul of Christ? That our broken tar-
nished bits of loyalty can make a difference to our
Redeemer?

In case we should not believe it, it is written clearly all
over the gospels. Why did He choose twelve men at the
first? "That they might be with Him," say the evangelists
simply, which means that somehow it helped Him in spite
of their blundering obtuseness, in some mysterious way it
encouraged Him to have those friends of His around Him.
And so through the last terrible week He kept returning
every night to the healing peace of the home at Bethany.

And so He asked Peter and James and John to stay beside Him in Gethsemane. And so, one feels sure, on the road to Calvary His love ran out toward Simon of Cyrene who eased His burden and carried His cross the last stage of that dreadful journey. And so, dying at last forsaken, there came to Him through the darkness and roar of the swellings of Jordan one tribute of recognition and devotion from a wretched creature hanging there beside Him, "Lord, in Thy kingdom remember me." I verily believe that, hearing that, Christ's heart leapt up, for it meant that He was not going out defeated and forsaken; that here was the beginning of the salvation of the world, and all God had promised from the travail of His soul was coming true already; here was the first installment of the final victory.

All these—the dying thief and the Cyrenian, the Bethany family, the blundering disciples, and this poor nameless leper with his grateful heart—were God's reinforcing messengers to the Lord Jesus Christ.

I ask again—did you realize that you could do something like that for the Christ who has done everything for you? That your gratitude and loyalty really mean much that to God?

And lest anyone should not quite know how to set about it or where to begin, let me remind you that Jesus Himself has made it very plain. "Inasmuch as you do it unto one of the least of these, you do it unto Me."

This is the dynamic motive of "Christian Aid." It is one thing to be temperamentally kindhearted by nature; but it is quite another thing to aid the suffering because you are seeing Christ stretching out His hands to you in every starving child, every war-victimized sufferer, every friend of your own who is unhappy or forlorn.

Dr. Theodore Ferris has told a story of a traveler out in Africa watching a nun dressing the wounds of a leper. The wounds were revolting, gruesome, and repulsive. As he watched her, he said, "I wouldn't do that for ten thousand dollars." She looked up at him, and said, "I wouldn't either." She was not doing it for all the dollars in the world. She was doing it for love, for gratitude to One who had loved her and given Himself for her. Inasmuch as you do it to one of the least, you do it unto Christ.

It is this unbounded love and gratitude which must be the motivating dynamic of Christian aid and action. In the memorable, moving words of Charles Kingsley in a letter to his wife: "Must we not thank, and thank, and thank forever, and toil and toil forever for Him?"

It would be a wonderful thing if from this congregation today, and from every Christian soul, there went up to God a great new surge of gratitude and thanksgiving. "Bless the Lord, O my soul, and forget not all His benefits" . . . who has crowned you with loving-kindness and tender mercy," who goes on daily loading you with gifts beyond all deserving—bless the Lord indeed! And, O my soul, turn your unpayable indebtedness into dedicated service, for the sake of those who need your help and for the love of Christ your Savior.

Genuine Worship Involves Feeling

Aiden Wilson Tozer (1897–1963) was a self-taught preacher and theologian whose sermons and writings have greatly influenced the church around the world with its emphasis on personal holiness and the importance of glorifying God. He pastored Christian and Missionary Alliance churches in West Virginia, Ohio, Pennsylvania, and Indiana before becoming pastor of the Southside Alliance Church in Chicago in 1928. When a heart attack called him home May 12, 1963, he was pastoring the Avenue Road Church in Toronto. For many years he edited *The Alliance Weekly*, later called *The Alliance Witness*, and his editorials have been compiled into many books.

This sermon is taken from *Whatever Happened to Worship?* by A. W. Tozer, published in 1985 by Christian Publications and edited by Gerald B. Smith.

Aiden Wilson Tozer

12

GENUINE WORSHIP INVOLVES FEELING

Acts 9:1–9

How long do you think it will be, if Jesus tarries, before some of the amazing new churches like those in the primitive Baliem Valley of Irian Jaya, Indonesia, will be sending gospel missionaries to Canada and the United States?

If that thought upsets you, you desperately need to read this chapter.

I have a reason for suggesting this as a possibility at some time in the future. In Chicago, I was introduced to a deeply serious Christian brother who had come from his native India with a stirring and grateful testimony of the grace of God in his life.

I asked him about his church background, of course. He was not Pentecostal. He was neither Anglican nor Baptist. He was neither Presbyterian nor Methodist.

He did not even know what we mean by the label, *interdenominational*. He was simply a brother in Christ.

This Indian had been born into the Hindu religion, but he was converted to and became a disciple of Jesus Christ by reading and seriously studying the New Testament record of the death and resurrection of our Lord.

He spoke English well enough to express his Christian concerns for the world and for the churches. I asked him to speak in my pulpit.

Through that encounter I realized that unless we arouse ourselves spiritually, unless we are brought back to genuine love and adoration and worship, our candlestick could be removed. We may need missionaries coming to us, indeed. We may need them to show us what genuine and vital Christianity is!

141

We should never forget that God created us to be joyful worshipers, but sin drew us into everything else but worship. Then in God's love and mercy in Christ Jesus, we were restored into the fellowship of the Godhead through the miracle of the new birth.

"You have been forgiven and restored," God reminds us. "I am your Creator and Redeemer and Lord, and I delight in your worship."

I don't know, my friend, how that makes you feel—but I feel that I must give God the full response of my heart. I am happy to be counted as a worshiper.

Well, that word *feel* has crept in here and I know that you may have an instant reaction against it. In fact, I have had people tell me very dogmatically that they will never allow "feeling" to have any part in their spiritual lives and experience. I reply, "Too bad for you!" I say that because I have voiced a very real definition of what I believe true worship to be: *worship is to feel in the heart!*

In the Christian faith, we should be able to use the word *feel* boldly and without apology. What worse thing could be said of us as the Christian church if it could be said that we are a feelingless people?

Worship must always come from an inward attitude. It embodies a number of factors, including the mental, spiritual, and emotional. You may not at times worship with the same degree of wonder and love that you do at other times, but the attitude and the state of mind are consistent if you are worshiping the Lord.

A husband and father may not appear to love and cherish his family with the same intensity when he is discouraged, when he is tired from long hours in business or when events have made him feel depressed.

He may not outwardly show as much love toward his family, but it is there, nonetheless, for it is not a feeling only. It is an attitude and a state of mind. It is a sustained act, subject to varying degrees of intensity and perfection.

I came into the kingdom of God with joy, knowing that I had been forgiven. I do know something of the emotional life that goes along with conversion to Christ.

I well remember, however, that in my early Christian fellowship, there were those who warned me about the dangers of "feeling." They cited the biblical example of Isaac feeling the arms of Jacob and thinking they were Esau's. Thus the man who went by his feelings was mistaken!

That sounds interesting, but it is not something on which you can build Christian doctrine.

Think of that sick woman in the gospel record who had had an issue of blood for twelve years and had suffered many things of many physicians.

Mark records that when she had heard of Jesus, she came in the throng and merely touched His garment. In the same instant "the fountain of her blood was dried up; and she felt in her body that she was healed of that plague" (Mark 5:29).

Knowing what had been done within her by the Savior, she "came and fell down before him, and told him all the truth" (5:33). Her testimony was in worship and praise. She felt in her body that she was healed.

Those of us who have been blessed within our own beings would not join in any crusade to "follow your feelings." On the other hand, if there is no feeling at all in our hearts, then we are dead!

If you wake up tomorrow morning and there is absolute numbness in your right arm—no feeling at all—you will quickly dial the doctor with your good left hand.

Real worship is, among other things, a feeling about the Lord our God. It is in our hearts. And we must be willing to express it in an appropriate manner.

We can express our worship to God in many ways. But if we love the Lord and are led by His Holy Spirit, our worship will always bring a delighted sense of admiring awe and a sincere humility on our part.

The proud and lofty man or woman cannot worship God any more acceptably than can the proud devil himself. There must be humility in the heart of the person who would worship God in spirit and in truth.

The manner in which many moderns think about worship makes me uncomfortable. Can true worship be engineered and manipulated? Do you foresee with me the time to come when churches may call the pastor a "spiritual engineer"?

I have heard of psychiatrists being called "human engineers," and of course, they are concerned with our heads. We have reduced so many things to engineering or scientific or psychological terms that the coming of "spiritual engineers" is a possibility. But this will never replace what I have called the astonished wonder wherever worshipers are described in the Bible.

We find much of spiritual astonishment and wonder in the book of Acts. You will always find these elements present when the Holy Spirit directs believing men and women.

On the other hand, you will not find astonished wonder among men and women when the Holy Spirit is not present.

Engineers can do many great things in their fields, but no mere human force or direction can work the mysteries of God among men. If there is no wonder, no experience of mystery, our efforts to worship will be futile. There will be no worship without the Spirit.

If God can be understood and comprehended by any of our human means, then I cannot worship Him. One thing is sure. I will never bend my knees and say "Holy, holy, holy" to that which I have been able to decipher and figure out in my own mind! That which I can explain will never bring me to the place of awe. It can never fill me with astonishment or wonder or admiration.

The philosophers called the ancient mystery of the personhood of God the *mysterium conundrum*. We who are God's children by faith call Him "our Father which art in heaven." In sections of the church where there is life and blessing and wonder in worship, there is also the sense of divine mystery. Paul epitomized it for us as "Christ in you, the hope of glory."

What does happen, then, in a Christian church when a fresh and vital working of the Spirit of God brings revival? In my study and observations, a revival generally results in a sudden bestowment of a spirit of worship. This is not the result of engineering or of manipulation. It is something God bestows on people hungering and thirsting for Him. With spiritual renewing will come a blessed spirit of loving worship.

These believers worship gladly because they have a high view of God. In some circles, God has been abridged, reduced, modified, edited, changed, and amended until He is no longer the God whom Isaiah saw, high and lifted up. Because He has been reduced in the minds of so many people, we no longer have that boundless confidence in His character that we used to have.

He is the God to whom we go without doubts, without fears. We know He will not deceive us or cheat us. He will not break His covenant or change His mind.

We have to be convinced so we can go into His presence in absolute confidence. In our hearts is this commitment, "Let God be true, but every man a liar" (Romans 3:4).

The God of the whole earth cannot do wrong! He does not need to be rescued. It is man's inadequate concept of God that needs to be rescued.

Thankfully, when God made us in His own image, He gave us the capability to appreciate and admire His attributes.

I once heard Dr. George D. Watson, one of the great Bible teachers of his generation, point out that men can have two kinds of love for God—the love of gratitude or the love of excellence. He urged that we go on from gratefulness to a love of God just because He is God and because of the excellence of His character.

Unfortunately, God's children rarely go beyond the boundaries of gratitude. I seldom hear anyone in worshipful prayer admiring and praising God for His eternal excellence.

Many of us are strictly "Santa Claus" Christians. We think of God as putting up the Christmas tree and putting our gifts underneath. That is only an elementary kind of love.

We need to go on. We need to know the blessing of worshiping in the presence of God without thought of wanting to rush out again. We need to be delighted in the presence of utter, infinite excellence.

Such worship will have the ingredient of fascination, of high moral excitement. Plainly, some of the men and women in the Bible knew this kind of fascination in their fellowship with God. If Jesus the Son is to be known and loved and served, the Holy Spirit must be allowed to illuminate our human lives. That personality will then be captured and entranced by the presence of God.

What is it that makes a human cry out:

> O Jesus, Jesus, dearest Lord!
> Forgive me if I say,
> For very love, Thy sacred name
> A thousand times a day.
>
> Burn, burn, O love, within my heart,
> Burn fiercely night and day,
> Till all the dross of earthly loves
> Is burned, and burned away.

Those expressions came from the worshiping heart of Frederick W. Faber. He was completely fascinated by all he had experienced in the presence and fellowship of a loving God and Savior. He was surely filled with an intensity of moral excitement. He was struck with wonder at the inconceivable magnitude and moral splendor of the Being whom we call our God.

Such fascination with God must necessarily have an element of adoration. You may ask me for a definition of adoration in this context. I will say that when we adore God, all of the beautiful ingredients of worship are brought to white, incandescent heat with the fire of the Holy Spirit. To adore God means we love Him with all the powers within us. We love Him with fear and wonder and yearning awe.

The admonition to "love the Lord thy God with all thy heart . . . and with all thy mind" (Matt. 22:37) can mean only one thing. It means to adore Him.

I use the word *adore* sparingly, for it is a precious word. I love babies and I love people, but I cannot say I adore them. Adoration I keep for the only One who deserves it. In no other presence and before no other being can I kneel in reverent fear and wonder and yearning and feel the sense of possessiveness that cries "Mine, mine!"

They can change the expressions in the hymnals, but whenever men and women are lost in worship they will cry out, "Oh God, thou art my God; early will I seek thee" (Ps. 63:1). Worship becomes a completely personal love experience between God and the worshiper. It was like that with David, with Isaiah, with Paul. It is like that with all whose desire has been to possess God.

This is the glad truth: God is *my* God.

Brother or sister, until you can say *God and I*, you cannot say *us* with any meaning. Until you have been able to meet God in loneliness of soul, just you and God— as if there was no one else in the world—you will never know what it is to love the other persons in the world.

In Canada, those who have written of the saintly Holy Anne said, "She talks to God as if there was nobody else but God and He had no other children but her." That was not a selfish quality. She had found the value and delight of pouring her personal devotion and adoration at God's feet.

Consecration is not difficult for the person who has met God. Where there is genuine adoration and fascination, God's child wants nothing more than the opportunity to pour out his or her love at the Savior's feet.

A young man talked to me about his spiritual life. He had been a Christian for several years, but he was concerned that he might not be fulfilling the will of God for his life. He spoke of coldness of heart and lack of spiritual power. I could tell that he was discouraged—and afraid of hardness of heart.

I gave him a helpful expression which has come from the writings of Bernard of Clairvaux: "My brother, only the heart is hard that does not know it is hard. Only he is hardened who does not know he is hardened. When we are concerned for our coldness, it is because of the yearning God has put there. God has not rejected us."

God puts the yearning and desire in our hearts, and He does not turn away and thus mock us. God asks us to seek His face in repentance and love and we then find all of His gracious fullness awaiting. In God's grace, that is a promise for the whole wide world.

You have read of Blaise Pascal, the famous seventeenth century French scientist often classed as one of the six great thinkers of all time. He was considered a genius in mathematics, and his scientific inquiry was broad. He was a philosopher and a writer. But best of all, he experienced a personal, overwhelming encounter with God one night that changed his life.

Pascal wrote on a piece of paper a brief account of his experience, folded the paper and kept it in a pocket close to his heart, apparently as a reminder of what he had felt. Those who attended him at his death found the worn, creased paper. In Pascal's own hand it read:

> From about half-past ten at night to about half-after midnight—fire! O God of Abraham, God of Isaac, God of Jacob—not the God of the philosophers and the wise. The God of Jesus Christ who can be known only in the ways of the Gospel. Security—feeling—peace—joy—tears of joy. Amen.

Were these the expressions of a fanatic, an extremist?

No. Pascal's mind was one of the greatest. But the living God had broken through and beyond all that was human and intellectual and philosophical. The astonished Pascal could only describe in one word the visitation in his spirit: "Fire!"

Understand that this was not a statement in sentences for others to read. It was the ecstatic utterance of a yielded man during two awesome hours in the presence of his God.

There was no human engineering or manipulation there. There was only wonder and awe and adoration wrought by the presence of the Holy Spirit of God as Pascal worshiped.

What we need among us is a genuine visitation of the Spirit. We need a sudden bestowment of the spirit of worship among God's people.

NOTES

The Beauty of the Lord

John Daniel Jones (1865–1942) served for forty years at the Richmond Hill Congregational Church in Bournemouth, England, where he ministered the Word with a remarkable consistency of quality and effectiveness, as his many volumes of published sermons attest. A leader in his denomination, he gave himself to church extension (he helped to start thirty new churches), assistance to needier congregations, and increased salaries for the clergy. He spoke at D. L. Moody's Northfield Conference in 1919.

This sermon is from his book, *The Hope of the Gospel*, published in 1911 by Hodder and Stoughton.

John Daniel Jones

13

THE BEAUTY OF THE LORD

And let the beauty of the Lord our God be upon us (Psalm 90:17).

"THE BEAUTY OF THE LORD OUR GOD." It was Charles Kingsley, was it not, who was overheard in his last illness murmuring quietly to himself, "How beautiful God is! How beautiful God is!" Perhaps the phrase, "the beauty of God," strikes us as just a little inappropriate and incongruous. We do not often apostrophize God as Augustine did—"O beauty, so old and yet so new, too late I loved Thee." And yet it must be true that God is beautiful. He is indeed the supreme and absolute beauty. The old Greeks put into their statues and representations of their gods their highest conceptions of human beauty; into their Aphrodite, all they knew of womanly charm; into their Apollo, all they knew of manly grace; into their Zeus, all they knew of royal majesty and dignity. The instinct that made them thus identify the divine with the beautiful was altogether right. It was only the mode of expression that was wrong. It was *physical* beauty they attributed to their deities, and they did this because their conception of deity was material and anthropomorphic. But the Godhead is not like unto silver or gold graven by art and man's device. God is a Spirit, and the beauty that characterizes Him is moral and spiritual beauty. You cannot express this beauty on canvas or in stone, but you can always feel it with the worshipful and believing heart.

From this point of view—that is, from the standpoint of beauty of character—how beautiful God is! You could guess as much from glancing at His works. I remember a friend of mine, after reading a chapter from, I believe, one of John Ruskin's works, remarking to me, "What a beautiful mind the man has!" And so exactly when I look out upon the works of God's hands I always feel moved to say, "What a beautiful mind God has!" Take the glory of the springtime. The earth in springtime fills anyone who has any sense of beauty with a perfect exhilaration of delight. It is full of light and fragrance and life and color. I look upon the trees dressed in their new robes of fresh and vivid green; I look upon the fields, decked as they are with innumerable white-eyed daisies and yellow butter-cups; I look at the wealth of color in our gardens; I listen to the joyous song of the birds; and when I remember that God is the Author and Giver of all this color, fragrance, glory, and song, I am constrained to cry with Kingsley, "How beautiful God is! How beautiful God is!"

But though *Nature* as our hymn puts it—

> With open volume stands
> To spread her Maker's praise abroad;
> And every labor of His hands
> Shows something worthy of a God,

it is not in nature that I find the highest revelation of the "beauty of the Lord." For that I turn to the gospel. You remember that passionate psalm in which the singer expresses his love for God's house—"One thing have I desired of the Lord," he cries, "that will I seek after, that I may dwell in the house of the Lord all the days of my life." And why did he desire this perpetual abiding in God's house? He himself supplies the answer: "To behold the beauty of the Lord." That was the attraction, the compelling fascination of the sanctuary—in it, as nowhere else, the psalmist beheld the pleasantness of the Lord, the delightsomeness of the character of God in all its perfection and completeness. And to the psalmist there was no vision comparable to this vision of the divine pleasantness; everything else was dust and ashes compared to this; like St. Paul, he counted all things but loss if only he could gaze upon God, and so he would fain dwell in the house of the Lord all the days of his life, that he might behold the beauty of the Lord. For it is in the sanctuary that the "pleasantness," the "beauty" of God's character is most clearly revealed. The heavens declare the glory of God—yes, but His Holy Word declares it more plainly still. And it is declared most plainly of all in the Incarnate Word—in Jesus Christ. If you want to behold the "beauty of the Lord," you can do better than study the book of nature; come and study Jesus Christ, for in Him dwells all the fullness of the Godhead bodily, and He and the Father are one.

Wherein the "Beauty" Consists

Now, I am going to ask the question wherein the beauty of the Lord, as revealed in Jesus Christ, consists. For "beauty" is itself always a *product*. It is not itself a single quality or characteristic; it is the result of a combination of qualities and characteristics. It is so even in the matter of *physical beauty*. I cannot discuss beauty as an artist could. But this I know, that regular features by themselves do not create beauty; and a fair complexion by itself does not create beauty; and a graceful carriage by itself does not create beauty. Beauty is a complex thing. It takes regularity of feature, brilliance of complexion, grace of carriage, and, above everything else, pleasantness of expression to create the impression of beauty. It is like the ray of light. The ray is really not single, though it seems such. It is complex. Let it fall upon a prism and it splits up into its constituent colors. It is a combination of violet and orange and green and blue that produces the purity and beauty of the white ray. And moral and spiritual beauty is also a complex thing. It is never the result of one quality but always of a combination of qualities. Beauty, in a word, is something that can be analyzed. You can see some of the necessary constituents of moral and spiritual beauty in most people's characters. But no human life ever lived on this earth has ever created the impression of perfect beauty. The combination is never complete. Some element or other is always lacking. There is ever some defect, some flaw, some fault. The only perfect and flawless beauty is the "beauty of the Lord." Now, I want to inquire what are the elements that go to make up the divine beauty. What are the constituents which, blended together, create the impression of the divine "pleasantness"? I am not going to mention all of them, for every good we know of is in God. I will confine myself to two qualities—contrasted qualities almost—which, blended together, go far toward creating the impression of the ineffable beauty of God.

And first I will mention *God's holiness*. There can be no moral beauty without holiness. It is in a very real sense the basal, the foundation quality of all moral character. When a man's life is smudged and stained with sin, the beauty of his character is wholly gone. Now, the Bible is full of an awe-stricken sense of the *holiness of God*. "The Lord our God is holy"—it was the first truth about the character of God that the Israelites were taught to learn. The contents of the law and the awe-inspiring circumstances that accompanied the giving of it were all meant to grave upon their hearts the truth of the "holiness of God." God is absolute, awful purity, that is almost the main lesson of the Old Testament. Before Him even the cherubim veil their faces in their wings and continually do cry, "Holy, holy, holy, is the Lord God of Hosts." So absolute is the holiness of God, that, compared with Him, even the whiteness of the angel's wing seems stained and soiled. And this quality of *holiness* is a permanent element in the beauty of the Lord. In Jesus Christ, He revealed Himself as the Holy One. Our Lord was the chiefest among ten thousand and the altogether lovely, and the basal element in His beauty is His holiness. "He did no sin, neither was guile found in His mouth." Perhaps in these days we are tempted to overlook, if not to ignore, this element in the divine beauty and glory. But there would be no beauty in God, He would indeed cease to be God, if He were not holy. The most striking feature in Swiss scenery, the glory and boast of Switzerland, is the vision of its mighty mountain peaks clothed ever in their mantles of snowy white. Take the snowy mountains away, and you have destroyed the beauty of Switzerland. And in much the same way you destroy the "beauty of the Lord" if you forget His holiness. The basal thing in God's character is His "awful purity." We need to lift our eyes to these shining and snow-clad peaks of the divine holiness if we are ever to be moved to say, "How beautiful God is!"

And the second quality in the character of God that I will mention is His *grace*. I have been saying that *holiness* is the basal element in moral beauty. I want to go on now to say that holiness in and by itself would not produce the impression of *beauty*. For the word "beauty" carries with it the suggestion of *charm*. Indeed, the word that is translated "beauty" might, perhaps, be more correctly translated "pleasantness." It is winsome and attractive beauty. It is not something that commands your admiration simply, it is something that constrains your love. Now, *holiness*, in and of itself, would scarcely constrain love. Nobody would think of describing those snow-clad peaks of Switzerland as "pleasant"—they are grand, if you like; majestic, if you like; awe-inspiring, if you like. And in the same way "holiness" by itself is not "pleasant"; it is too high and majestic and austere; it does not charm and win us; it awes us, it subdues us—I might almost say it terrifies us. "Woe is me, for I am a man of unclean lips," is the heart-broken cry of the prince of the prophets. It was a cry wrung from him by a vision of the holiness of God. "Depart from me, for I am a sinful man, O Lord," is the bitter cry of the chief of the apostles. It was a cry wrung from him by a vision of the holiness of God. There is something more than *holiness* needed to create the beauty that wins and charms and attracts. And that something more we find in God's *grace*. The holiness of God would compel our reverence and awe; but the grace of God wins our love.

That was what struck the disciples most about the character of Jesus. "We beheld his glory," says John; "glory as of the only begotten from the Father, full of grace." It was this characteristic of Jesus that gave Him His charm. "Publicans and sinners," we read, "came together for to hear Him." It was His *grace* that attracted them. "The common people heard him gladly." It was His *love* that drew them. "The grace of Christ"—the stooping, condescending, love of Christ—how it shines forth in the gospel story! Read the account of the wedding at Cana—

what delicate considerateness Christ showed! Read the
story of His visit to the house of Zacchaeus—what infinite
compassion and beautiful hopefulness He displayed! Read
the narrative of His dealings with the woman who was a
sinner—what a depth of tenderness and forgiving love
He revealed! And these are the things that lent charm
and winsomeness to the character of Jesus. No wonder
the common people delighted to hear Him; no wonder
publicans and sinners hung on His words and followed
Him from place to place—He was full of grace. Mere holiness would not have drawn them. Righteousness is apt to
be hard and repellent. You remember what Paul says:
"Scarcely for a righteous man will one die"; there is not
much about the righteous man to command enthusiastic
love. The righteous man is often harsh and austere. "But
for a good man," he says, "some would even dare to die."
When righteousness is blended with love to produce goodness, then people's hearts are won to such enthusiastic
devotion that they will even dare to die. And that is what
you find in Jesus—love has joined hands with righteousness to produce goodness. And Jesus Christ in this is but
the picture and expression of God. God is more than
infinite holiness; He is also boundless love. He is more
than the pure God who cannot behold iniquity; He is the
loving God who gave His Son to die to save the sinner.
And that constitutes the beauty, the pleasantness of the
Lord; in Him mercy and truth have met together, righteousness and peace have kissed each other.

The Beauty of God a Human Possession

And now, having spoken thus briefly about the "beauty
of the Lord," I want to call your attention to the prayer
the psalmist utters in the text. He prays, "Let the beauty
of the Lord our God be upon us." He prays, in a word, that
the divine beauty and glory may become the possession of
all God's people. This is a daring prayer. Is it a possible
prayer? Is it a prayer that can be answered and realized?
Yes, surely it can. It was one of the best-beloved of our
modern mystics who said in his own quaint way, "The
Christian ought always to be good-looking." Beneath the

quaint phrase there lies a great and blessed truth. The Christian ought always to be good-looking. He ought to share in the perfect beauty of God. "Let the beauty of the Lord our God be upon us." It is no vain and impossible wish. It is no foolish and unwarranted prayer. People have shared in the glory of God. There have been those on whom, visibly and unmistakably, the beauty of God has rested. The apostle tells us that all who steadfastly gaze upon the glory of the Lord are transformed into the same image from glory to glory. And the apostle's statement is confirmed and ratified by the facts of experience. People have been so changed and transformed. "And they took knowledge of them," I read about Peter and John, "that they had been with Jesus." They had caught from their Master some of the "beauty of the Lord." "And all that sat in the council," I read about Stephen, "fastening their eyes on him, saw his face as it had been the face of an angel." Stephen had caught some of the "beauty of the Lord." "From henceforth let no man trouble me," says St. Paul; "I bear in my body the marks of the Lord Jesus"—"the marks of the Lord Jesus," not simply in the scars and wounds he had suffered in his Christian service, but even more in his consecration and devotion and absolute self-sacrifice; and all this was Paul's share of the "beauty of the Lord."

And to come from those early days down to these days of ours, there are men and women in our midst who are invested with this heavenly beauty. "I have seen God in you," a famous novelist makes one of her characters say of another; "I have seen God in you." The human life was glorified with some of the "beauty of the Lord." No, this is no wild, extravagant, and impossible prayer. The "beauty of the Lord" is a beauty in which we may all share. The New Testament quite clearly contemplates our sharing in this beauty. In the beauty of *holiness*, to begin with, for St. Peter says, "Like as he which called you is holy, be ye yourselves also holy in all manner of living, because it is written, Ye shall be holy, for I am holy." And in the beauty of love, for St. Paul says, "Let this mind be in you which was also in Christ Jesus," and the "mind which was in

Christ Jesus" was, as the apostle proceeds to show, the gracious, unselfish, loving, and self-sacrificing mind illustrated in the Cross. The *grace* of the Lord Jesus Christ is to be with us.

The New Testament clearly contemplates our sharing in the holiness and love of God. The "beauty of the Lord our God" is to be upon us. But is it? Do we share in it? Have we some of the holiness of God? Do we participate, to some poor degree, in the divine purity? And have we the loving mind of Christ? And does the combination of holiness and love make people feel that the beauty of the Lord our God is upon us? I repeat once more, we may share in the very beauty of God; but, I am bound to add, it is not a beauty easily or cheaply won. This is a costly beauty, and it is not to be acquired without paying the price.

Holiness is costly. Everyone who has sought to acquire it knows this. It costs struggle and agony and blood and tears. "We wrestle," says the apostle, "not against flesh and blood, but against the principalities, against the powers, against the world-rulers of this darkness, against the spiritual hosts of wickedness in the heavenly places"— that terrific struggle is the price of holiness. "If thy hand cause thee to stumble, cut it off; it is good for thee to enter into life maimed rather than having thy two hands to go into hell; and if thy foot cause thee to stumble, cut it off; it is good for thee to enter into life halt rather than having thy two feet to be cast into hell. And if thine eye cause thee to stumble, cast it out; it is good for thee to enter into the kingdom of God with one eye, rather than having two eyes to be cast into hell." And this maiming and cutting, this lopping off of the hand and the foot, this plucking-out of the eye represents the price and cost of holiness.

And if holiness is *costly*, so also is the *grace of love*. See what it cost God. It cost Him His only Son. Calvary stands for the cost of love to God. And Calvary stands for ever as the type and illustration of the costliness of love. For *love* implies a cross and a crucifixion. Love implies the crucifixion of self, the absolute putting away and annihilation of self. Therefore Jesus said, "Whosoever would come after

Me, let him take up his cross, deny himself daily and follow Me." The cross—that is the price of love. Yes, without doubt, this is a costly beauty. But it is worth the price. All other beauty is like a fading flower. Age wrinkles the fairest brow, takes the color out of the brightest cheek, bends the straightest and most graceful form; but age cannot wither "the beauty of the Lord." It grows ever more and more beautiful as the years pass. The only change is a change "from glory to glory." And it ends in the perfect and complete beauty of heaven. "We shall be like Him, for we shall see Him as He is." I ask, once again, do you possess this fadeless and heavenly beauty? Physical beauty is beyond the reach of many of us; but "the beauty of the Lord our God" may become the possession of us all. If we commune with Christ, if we take up our cross and follow Christ, we shall be transformed into His image from glory to glory.

The Effect of This Beauty on the World.

In the last place, notice the effect of *the divine beauty upon the world.* If only the beauty of the Lord our God is upon us, the world will be startled, charmed, subdued. There is no such apologetic for Christianity as a beautiful Christian life. A holy and loving character is the most potent and effective of all sermons. Perhaps that is why Christianity has made such slow progress—there has been so little of the beauty of the Lord our God upon us. There has been so little holiness; there has been so little love. There has been so little difference between us and those of the world. We have been selfish, grasping, loveless, as they are. The world is so indifferent to the charm of Christianity because it has seen so little of it. But whenever people see Christian people with some of the beauty of the Lord upon them, they are subdued and won.

I read about the members of the early church, in the spirit of love, selling their goods and contributing to one another's needs, continuing steadfastly in the prayers and taking their simple food with gladness and singleness of heart, praising God; and the result of it all was "they found favor with all the people." All Jerusalem was impressed by the vision, in the characters of these first Christians, of "the beauty of the Lord." I read about a young Glasgow engineer who joined a Glasgow church, and who, when asked what it was that had won him for Christ, replied that it was the impression produced upon him by the life and character of the foreman in his shop. He had been won by the "beauty of the Lord" in a human life. And that is what I believe is most sorely wanted in order to conquer the world for our Lord—that the beauty of the Lord our God should be upon us all.

A significant sentence follows this one of the text: "Let the beauty of the Lord our God be upon us: establish thou the work of our hands upon us; yea, the work of our hands, establish thou it." That is a striking sequence— *first* the "beauty of the Lord," *then* "the established work." *First* the Christian character, *then* the success of our labors. We cannot have the second without the first. There can be no triumph for the Christian church until all Christians are clothed in the beauty of the Lord. But if only the beauty of the Lord were upon us, our work would be speedily established. "If those who call themselves Christians only lived the Christian life," said Charles Kingsley, "the world would be converted to God in a day." We long to see our work established; we long to see church and school crowned with success; we long to see the kingdoms of the world becoming the kingdoms of our God and of His Christ. But there is a prior prayer we need to offer. The secret of the slow progress is in ourselves. We are such unlovely Christians. We do not commend the gospel we profess. Let us ask God to do His work first upon us—to purge us of our littlenesses and selfishnesses and sins, to make us holy and pure and loving. Yes, let us pray that, whatever the price and cost, "the beauty of the Lord our God" may be upon us; then will God also establish the work of our hands upon us; yea, the work of our hands He will establish it.